Mike Figgis began his career as a musician, playing with various bands before studying music in London. He then joined the experimental performance art group The People Show and toured with them for ten years before founding his own company. After failing to gain a place at the NFTS (where he now teaches occasionally) he began making short films and this led to a second career in a more mainstream environment.

His film credits include *Stormy Monday*, *Internal Affairs*, the award-winning *Leaving Las Vegas*, as well as the innovative digital films *Timecode* and *Hotel*.

After fifteen years in the Hollywood system Figgis moved back to London where he divides his time between film-making, photography and music.

The 36
Dramatic Situations

MIKE FIGGIS

Date: 10/19/17

FABER & FABER

First published in the UK in 2017
First published in the USA in 2017
by Faber & Faber Ltd
Bloomsbury House
74–77 Great Russell Street
London WC1B 3DA

Typeset by Faber & Faber Ltd
Printed and bound by CPI Group (UK) Ltd, Croydon CR0 4YY

The right of Mike Figgis to be identified as author of this work
has been asserted in accordance with Section 77 of the Copyright,
Designs and Patents Act 1988

A CIP record for this book
is available from the British Library

ISBN 978–0–571–30504–9

FSC
www.fsc.org
MIX
Paper from
responsible sources
FSC® C020471

10 9 8 7 6 5 4 3 2 1

to Georges Polti

CONTENTS

VII

INTRODUCTION

Each genre of narrative storytelling has its limitations and advantages. The development of the novel opened up complex psychological possibilities. In the reader's mind the text is immediately translated into imagery via the 'internal cinema' of the brain. The sophisticated marriage of language and personal visualisation make the novel the most complex and interesting of all genres.

Theatre, with its somewhat limited range of visual effects and staging, has to rely heavily on the spoken word (of the actors, already a translation of the writer's intention). Consequently, narratives have to be simpler and shorter so as not to bore an already restless audience expecting to be entertained. Theatre borrows something from the novel. It expects the audience to add their own internal contribution to the drama. The sets may look fake, but with a little imagination and half-closed eyes we can allow ourselves to be seduced by the actor's reading of the text.

Cinema arrived and, with its innovative techniques and larger-than-life image, dragged theatre into a new reality. At its birth cinema attempted to film theatre, and then, as it took on board one technological innovation after another, quickly moved away from these limited techniques and began attempting to emulate the novel, converting its 'internal cinema' into a visually rich celluloid experience. It is difficult to imagine the impact early cinema must have had on audiences because moving imagery and visual effects have become so much a part of our experience from birth. It's almost impossible to imagine a world without this eye candy.

However, cinema still has one problem when compared to the novel: once a film actor is chosen, the character, for better or worse, will always have that actor's face, whereas the novel will always have the individual casting of the reader and is thus far more flexible. Each reader is having a unique experience.

But the cinema is the winner in every other sense, mainly because of its size and its brightness. In the Olympics of the senses, the eye will always win. Humans are programmed so that our eyes feed the bulk of the information to the brain, supported by sound, smell and touch. Whether we like it or not, we will always be seduced first and foremost by big bright pictures (and also small bright pictures like on the iPhone).

Earlier this year I had a productive meeting with a Hollywood studio and agreed to write an original script based upon a few ideas: namely, a contemporary LA story, a thriller with a female protagonist. I'd always enjoyed the blank canvas of LA for film, and the thriller is a very malleable genre for writers.

The first stage was to deliver a treatment that put these basic notions into a plot structure. A deadline was agreed that gave me about seven days to come up with something. The quick timing was my idea: I wanted to see just how the studio would react to something a bit more concrete than a pitch.

All writers have their own systems for writing. Mine is very simple: I do nothing until the very last moment. The word 'nothing' is, in this context, misleading. I fill my time with menial tasks: I iron shirts, rearrange the furniture – anything that allows the imagination to float unhindered.

I try to fake a dream state where the brain actually knows what it has to do and can get on with it. It works for me because my brain is working on the ideas unfettered by the limitations of the formal writing process.

And so, as my deadline got ever closer as I decided to tidy up all my bookshelves and get rid of the books which no longer deserved space and would thus make room for the piles of newer books on the floor. I came across a slim green paperback entitled *The 36 Dramatic Situations* by Georges Polti. A distant bell rang in the memory department: maybe a student gave the book to me? I did remember having resolved to read the book (long forgotten, obviously), so I began flicking through the pages and then reading the book from cover to cover. It appealed to my belief in serendipity and the Jungian idea of chance: I was about to write a story and here was a book on dramatic-writing technique. (I was also tickled by the fact that anagrams of POLTI are I PLOT and PILOT.)

I began looking up some of the references that accompany each of Polti's 'situations'. The Internet was a vital tool, and it became clear that the majority of the examples in the book were from long-forgotten writers (aside from obvious authors like Shakespeare and Dumas) and that therefore it was difficult to understand the references. I wondered how Polti's ideas would hold up within the genre of cinema. I started to make notes. As my writing became more detailed, my interest blossomed.

I made a graph of the 36 situations and then began adding selected films to see how the Polti method would react to cinema. It was immediately fascinating. I submitted all of my own films (those which I had been the writer of) and could see how very few of the 36 situations I had used repeatedly.

This proved to be the case with the work of other directors too. Which, of course, makes complete sense. It was the maestro Luis Buñuel who, in his book *My Last Breath*, talked about the few childhood experiences that shaped his creative thought and how he (and all of us) revisited those images and ideas time and time again. But Buñuel and the other greats of cinema would wrap these ideas in bizarre plot twists. In order to be able to do this, we writers need to be reminded periodically of the bigger picture of drama.

As I translated the Polti situations from the genre of theatre into cinema, it opened up a debate in my notebook: namely, what are the crucial differences between the two forms?

How Different Are They & Why Are They Different?

Let's begin with a banal question. Why would we want to go to a public space, sit in the dark with strangers and watch a group of men and women pretend to be characters in situations that clearly are not real, faking love, death, jealousy, hatred and sex? Put like that, it does seem decidedly odd, does it not?

But drama has existed for a long time and would seem to be an integral part of all cultures. I believe it exists for a profound reason, and ultimately this has almost nothing to do with the concept of entertainment. Drama exists because we need it. We need a public forum within which fundamental issues can be discussed: basically, the issues of mortality, and the big one, 'Is this all there is?'

Theatre developed as an excellent forum for these debates, and the basic issues were placed within the context of 'stories'.

But the limitations of theatre are self-evident. Finding a balance between intimacy, economics and the size of the audience quickly curtailed the possibilities and, by necessity, created a specific style of 'theatre' acting. In a large theatre (400-plus people) anyone sitting anywhere other than in the front rows is going to see the stage as a single image containing a set and people – what we in cinema call a wide shot. Consequently, the style of acting has to acknowledge that physical fact. Voices need to be artificially projected, emotional gestures need to be amplified (to see this at its worst, watch any opera) and the physical scenery can be moved only at specific breaks in a scene. Great theatre actors have managed to transcend these crude limitations and theatre does have one big ace up its sleeve . . .

INTIMACY. The connection with the audience is vital. If you think about an audience in a theatre and an audience in a cinema, this becomes very clear. It's unimaginable for a theatre spectator to be eating, making phone calls, going to the bathroom, etc. (although in recent times these habits have started to occur in live theatre as well as in cinema).

When I began writing this book, I wanted to find the one essential factor that defined the difference between cinema and theatre. I asked many people the same question, and the answers included:

In a play the performances will be slightly different every night

In theatre there is a live audience reacting to live actors

In cinema the scenery changes all of the time

... etc., etc. While all of this is true, it didn't have enough impact for me to justify the claim that cinema was actually a different genre altogether. Then I read the following quote from Ingmar Bergman:

Cinema is the ongoing exploration of the human face.

... and I was home! The use of the close-up is ultimately the main difference between cinema and theatre. It allows us to explore the human face in minute detail, to give us insight into the complex psychology of a character in a way that could never be possible in the theatre.

We study faces (portraits, photographs) so intently. We search the physical structure of the face to try to link what we know about the person. We use emotive phrases, like 'mean eyes', 'a cruel mouth', 'a kind face', 'shifty eyes', 'a cold expression', 'a sensual mouth', 'a blank stare', etc.

A thousand people can sit together in a cinema and study a massive close-up of an actor's face.

Let us imagine a dramatic moment and discuss how it would be dealt with in a theatre and in a cinema.

Husband and wife talking over dinner. Infidelity is in the air, perhaps one of them is having an affair. Their conversation seems innocent but is in fact laced with subtle questions about domestic trivia. Finally, the wife takes a deep breath and . . .

WIFE:

Are you having an affair?

HUSBAND:

What? What are you talking about? Don't be so silly.

If I were directing this moment for theatre, it would have to be exaggerated by the physical movements of the actors. Their gestures would have to be slightly larger than life (the husband almost chokes on his ratatouille) and their voices, in order to be heard at the back of the theatre, would certainly have to be louder than they should be in such an intimate environment. Theatre actors are taught these techniques (or they learn from necessity), and the best of them make it almost believable.

But in cinema I would almost certainly want to go to the opposite extreme and underplay everything because I know that *all of the emotion would be evident in the close-up*. Minute movements of the eyes, facial muscles and mouth would tell me everything I needed to know. Add to this the intimacy of the sound, the close recording of the voices, and you have a genre of hyper-intimacy that would be impossible to achieve on the stages of the National Theatre. In fact, it is interesting to note just how many theatre productions now opt for some use of video and audio technology within those traditional proscenium arches.

One of the first things I learned from experience as a film director was that the usual way of shooting a scene was to begin with the wide shot, then move into a medium one, before ending with the close-up. Actors always saved their emotions for the close-up, knowing full well that the editor would be using it as the pay-off for the scene.

Armed with this specific evaluation of 'What is cinema?' I began to look at Polti's book in a different way. I realised that quite a few adjustments would have to be made if I were to make his ideas work for cinema.

Cinema has opened up and expanded the idea of drama significantly, and a cine version of *The 36 Dramatic Situations* would need to reflect this. The book was published in France in 1895, but today the world is a very different place, with radical changes in ideas about race, gender, religion, family and sexuality. On the other hand, it is clear that most of the issues that drama dealt with then are still key issues now.

Cinema itself seems to be in a constant state of flux, particularly over the last ten years. Film-making technology has changed the scene so radically that new forms of film are appearing regularly and when it comes to the creative palette there is a large menu to choose from. Something as basic as whether the film will be in colour or black and white has a huge impact on the audience. Will the camera be static or moving? Will there be music to add to the drama? What kind of music? Will the editing be intrusive or passive? All these things have to be considered when making a film/drama and, therefore, also have to be factored into a cine version of *The 36 Dramatic Situations*.

The Cards

Chance has always been my friend. The first two films I made would never have happened without the intervention of chance and coincidence.

While I was writing this book I made 36 cards to remind myself of the situations, much as I would when structuring a script. One day I found myself holding the cards . . . as a pack! I had the overwhelming desire to shuffle, which I did, and then I randomly chose three cards. I pondered on a possible sequence and then drew another two cards. This was the moment of revelation for me. Let me explain . . .

Whenever I write a story there is a certain point when I get bogged down. I find the possibilities diminish as I progressively become the victim of a combination of the three-act structure and my own limited human experiences. I can no longer see the wood for the trees. Taking my chances with the cards enables me to open my mind to other possibilities. When I ponder these alternative ideas, I find that my mind has opened up and solutions present themselves – not necessarily the options on the cards, though I'm certainly influenced by them. Having experimented with quite a large number of volunteers over the last year, the results have often been quite startling. Jung wrote an amazing introduction to the *I Ching* in which he talks about chance, so none of my results particularly surprised me. Ultimately, I see the book and the cards primarily as useful stimuli to the imagination of the writer.

Going back to the *I Ching*, the interpretations are deliberately very expansive and poetic, and I suggest the same is true with my 36 situations. In Polti's original, he was much more definitive in his categories, but cinema is a more poetic medium (potentially) than theatre, and I recommend a looser interpretation. If we go along with Bergman's suggestion that 'Cinema is the ongoing exploration of the human face' (which in turn is the window to the soul), then we can assume that in a film we are exploring an interior dialogue. Polti wrote his book for the theatre, which is more concerned with the outer world. What is fascinating about the 36 situations is that, for me, they work for both the outer and inner worlds.

While I was creating the film chart, I realised just how subjective the interpretation of films can be. Three different people may interpret a film in very different ways. Situation 6, **DISASTER**, can be literally interpreted as a war or an earthquake or the sinking of the *Titanic*. But in a smaller, more intimate love story, it could be a case of unrequited love: the loved one marries another person, a personal, internal disaster of the highest magnitude. The main difference would be that a natural disaster would affect many people, whereas an internal disaster would affect only one person.

The 20th century gave us cinema and psychoanalysis, and our dramas became much more internal, so my 36 situations needed to reflect this. For example, situation 36, **LOSS OF A LOVED ONE**, was originally meant to mean the death of a loved one. I chose to interpret it as (also) the loss of a love, the inability to be with a person whom you love. Similarly, (23) **NECESSITY OF SACRIFICING LOVED ONES** need not be literal but rather the deliberate choice of walking away from a great love for family reasons or other complications. For example, in **Sophie's Choice** the character has to decide which of her children must die in order to save the other.

In Polti's time the family was a much more powerful institution, and eight of the situations deal with this. While ideas of family remain central to our codes and values, I would also suggest they can widen to include close-knit groups of friends or work colleagues. Statistically, we now spend more time at work, so (4) **REVENGE CONTAINED WITHIN A FAMILY** could also work with this wider interpretation, as could (13) **ENMITY OF KINSMEN**.

Some Small Changes to
the Original Sequence of Situations

There are two situations that are particularly relevant to cinema but rarely used in theatre, so Polti does not mention them. Therefore, I have taken the bold step of adding them to the 36. In order to make space (I didn't want to end up with 38 situations) I combined two of the original ones within existing categories. My new categories are:

COINCIDENCE
Film is the perfect medium for the setting up of chance meetings and events. Through editing, the audience participates in the process.

EXAMPLE:
(1) We see a man getting off a train and exiting the station. He is walking from the left of the screen to the right.
(2) We see a woman walking briskly in a busy street. She is walking from the right of the screen to the left.
(3) Add music, some tension.

After a series of edits between the two characters, it seems inevitable that they will bump into each other. After some brief dialogue establishing that they have not seen each other for ten years and that there is some dark history between them, we have created a plot with potential for development. This is pure cinema. The same idea would never work in the theatre. I felt it had to be included as a very useful device for the writer.

DREAM STATE

The techniques of cinema were very quickly put to work on the exploration of the mind.

```
EXAMPLE:
Buñuel's early films (L'Age d'or and Un Chien
andalou) have become benchmarks and helped to
create a visual dream language. Again, this is
something uniquely cinematic, not inherited from
theatre, and it deserves its own category.
```

In order to fit these two new ideas into the 36 I have combined (19) **SLAYING OF AN UNRECOGNISED FAMILY MEMBER** into (7) **CRUELTY AND MISFORTUNE**; and (18) **INVOLUNTARY CRIMES OF LOVE** is now included in (26) **INCEST** (formerly **CRIMES OF LOVE**).

Choice of Film Examples

To a large extent I have referred to films that have influenced me over the years. In some cases I use the same film over and over again to illustrate several different situations and how one situation may usefully interact with another. Thus:

```
L'Enfer (Claude Chabrol, 1994) illustrates:
(16) MADNESS
(32) MISTAKEN JEALOUSY
```

Festen (Thomas Vinterberg, 1998) illustrates:

  (4) **REVENGE CONTAINED WITHIN A FAMILY**

(26) **INCEST**

(27) **DISCOVERY OF THE DISHONOUR OF A LOVED ONE**

(33) **ERRONEOUS JUDGEMENT**

How I Use the Situations When Analysing a Film

EXAMPLE:

Don't Look Now (Nic Roeg, 1973)
After the death by drowning of their only
daughter, a married couple go to Venice to try to
make a new start. Strange events lead the wife
to believe that the daughter is trying to make
contact with them, but as the narrative proceeds
they are drawn into a dark, fateful cycle leading
to the murder of the husband at the hands of a
serial killer.

I marked the film as follows:

  (6) **DISASTER**. The loss of an only child.

(11) **THE ENIGMA**. Is the child really trying to make
      contact? Who is the child-like figure in the red coat
      sporadically seen in the back streets of Venice?

(16) **MADNESS**. The tragic death of the child affects the
      mother so much that she seems to lose her mind,
      hallucinating and imaging things.

(17) **FATAL IMPRUDENCE**. The father sees the small figure
      in the red coat and decides to follow. He is then led
      into a remote small street, at which point the film
      reveals the killer.

(18) **COINCIDENCE**. The film has a series of coincidences
    which allow the plot to develop.

(19) **DREAM STATE**. The husband imagines he sees his wife
    on a funeral barge. In fact, she is not there.

(35) **RECOVERY OF A LOST ONE**. The wife wants to believe
    that she can somehow resurrect the lost child. The
    husband thinks he sees the child scurrying through
    the dark streets in her red coat.

(36) **LOSS OF A LOVED ONE**. The narrative is built upon
    this situation, which begins the film. It also ends the
    film because the husband is killed and, therefore, the
    wife again loses a loved one.

The chart of films is fascinating. I see it as aesthetic DNA.
No two films use the exact same situations or sequence. This
is also reassuring for the screenwriter because it reminds
us that there is originality in the retelling of our common
experiences.

Suggestions for Using the System

(1) Where in the drama does the situation occur?

(2) Is it the 'motivating situation' or is it causing another
    situation to change?

(3) There are degrees of strength to each situation. Most
    dramas can be reduced to a small number of situations,
    but others use many.

(4) Ultimately, this book is meant to stimulate your
    imagination, to take you out of the narrow confines of
    conventional plot schemes and one's own experiential
    limitations.

(5) Be aware of gender issues in the 21st century. Try to break away from the clichés of male storytelling. When creating a new character, consider it male rather than female, or vice versa, and you may surprise yourself. A banal male/female cliché can become more interesting when the genders are reversed.

(6) Plot-driven stories use many situations in a creative way. Introducing more places and people into a story will invariably require the use of more situations than . . .

(7) . . . psychological dramas, which can have much simpler plot structures.

Some truly great films use very few of the situations – **La Dolce Vita** uses only five (5, 11, 23, 28, 36), **Brief Encounter** uses five (18, 21, 23, 28, 36) – while **Cool Hand Luke** uses 16 (1, 2, 3, 5, 7, 8, 9, 12, 13, 17, 20, 24, 27, 31, 35, 36). This indicates whether the narrative of the film is more concerned with the inner psychology of the characters, or whether the plot has many twists and turns. In the case of **Blue Velvet**, David Lynch uses 14 situations (1, 2, 5, 7, 9, 10, 11, 16, 17, 18, 19, 27, 28, 35) to create a dream world that somehow mirrors the cliché of the domestic thriller.

When making the film chart, I narrowed my choices down to 150 films. Many of them are well-known classics, while others are more obscure but, in my opinion, strong examples of the craft of cinema writing. A crude analysis of the chart revealed the following data.

THE TEN MOST USED SITUATIONS

(12) **OBTAINING** – 56 per cent

(31) **CONFLICTS WITH POWER** – 52 per cent

(17) **FATAL IMPRUDENCE** was used by 50 per cent

(9) **BRAVE ADVENTURE** – 48 per cent

(3) **REVENGE FOLLOWING A CRIME** – 48 per cent

(28) **OBSTACLES TO LOVE** – 46 per cent

(2) **DELIVERANCE** – 44 per cent

(5) **THE PURSUED** – 43 per cent

(7) **CRUELTY AND MISFORTUNE** – 40 per cent

(11) **THE ENIGMA** – 38 per cent

THE FIVE LEAST USED SITUATIONS

(26) **INCEST** – 4 per cent

(32) **MISTAKEN JEALOUSY** – 5 per cent

(14) **RIVALRY WITHIN A FAMILY** – 9 per cent

(19) **DREAM STATE** – 10 per cent

(21) **SELF-SACRIFICE FOR FAMILY** – 10 per cent

P.S. This all began with me putting off the moment of having to write a treatment. That moment inevitably arrived, and I'd left myself eight hours to come up with a good plot. I sat down with my pen and notebook and the ideas flowed easily and quickly. I found (of course) that I was using situations that were definitely outside of my usual landscape. For me *The 36 Dramatic Situations* were already proving to be an amazing tool.

P.P.S. I have just returned from another trip to LA, where I proposed a TV series based entirely upon the use of the cards. The Network has accepted the proposal, and I am in the process of writing it. It seems there is life in the cards. Good luck.

1. SUPPLICATION

SUPPLICATION: *the action of asking or begging for something earnestly or humbly: 'he fell to his knees in supplication'.*

Synonyms: *entreaty, plea, appeal, petition, solicitation, exhortation, urge, prayer, invocation, request.*

```
EXAMPLE:
Inception (Christopher Nolan, 2010)
A fugitive, Cobb, humbles himself to his Japanese
boss in order to return to his children in America.
```

Supplication can take several forms, and the act itself can either have redemptive power or be an act of humiliation.

Possible Scenarios

(1) A fugitive asks for help. In most dramas the 'fugitive' has the sympathy of the audience. He/she may be falsely accused or have committed a crime in order to protect someone. We will probably have had time to get to know the character and form sympathy, so the supplication would probably take place some time into the drama. It would be more unusual if we were either:

(a) unfamiliar with the supplicant; or

(b) unsympathetic to the supplicant, in which case we might feel, 'He made others suffer, now it is his turn.'

ANOTHER POSSIBILITY: were this situation to occur at the beginning of a drama, before we know any backstory, we would have to judge the truth of the supplicant based entirely on the performance of the actor. We would be part of the group that was being appealed to. Therefore, the psychology of the scene would be very different than if the scene were at the middle or end of the narrative, by which time we would have formed opinions about the character. In which case we might think:

(a) he/she is up to their old tricks, a con artist that will never reform; or

(b) the character has changed and, after turmoil, has arrived at a different place.

Specific to (b), the fugitives have to convince a group of strangers who may already have information about them that they're worthy of the group's charity. They must be sympathetic and able to convince the group, probably change their preconceptions. This sometimes comes about with the help of one member of the group of strangers – 'Perhaps he is telling the truth after all' – who then slowly manages to convince the others, one by one.

(2) Person exiled from a group begs them for help. A person behaves in a way that gravely alienates them from a group. We may sympathise with either the group or the individual.

At some point a situation develops and the individual realises that without the help of the group, they will be in trouble. Pride must be swallowed, followed by a humbling encounter and a plea for forgiveness.

If we are on the side of the supplicant, we feel the humiliation, take it personally on their behalf. If we sympathise with the group, we may enjoy the humbling of the individual. But either way, we are aware that this humiliation may lead to a desire for **REVENGE**.

Only rarely will we see the situation as positive, i.e. the individual has matured, learned something positive from the group ethic. This may typically occur in drama that is propagandist, political or religious, in situations where the human spirit is regarded as controllable by dogma or collective thought. Outside of these genres it is rare.

A key element would be whether the audience believes the subject is being truthful . . . or merely pretending to be humble. If truthful, it would signify that the individual has made a decision, arrived at a certain point and decided to alter their path.

(3) Character seeks pardon from a higher office. This is more formal, perhaps there's some kind of legal basis, working within a tighter set of rules and codes. Therefore, the drama would have to reflect this and the emotional content is more compressed. The narrative is more like a game in which the winner may be the side that manipulates the rules in the smartest way. Often in these scenarios the supplicant may be the

loser, a victim of a system that is impersonal and bound by inflexibility. The audience will almost certainly be sympathetic to the supplicant, who by now may be in an even worse position than before.

The psychology shifts depending on where this supplication is placed within the plot:

(a) beginning – now the character needs to begin from zero and rebuild a life, with the possibility of failure ever present;

(b) middle – things can improve or get worse; or

(c) end – it's over for the character, it's fatalistic, life is a huge struggle and in the end you lose.

EXAMPLE:

The Mission (Roland Joffé, 1986)
Conquistador Rodrigo Mendoza is torn by guilt for killing his own brother. He supplicates himself by climbing a mountain on his hands and knees, and is forgiven by the native Indians he has previously enslaved.

(4) Supplicant seeks pardon from a leader. The supplicant has to meet a boss, maybe a gang leader, to beg forgiveness for some breach of gang law. Only the boss can make the decision to forgive, and if he does, most probably there will be a price to pay for the gesture. In some way the supplicant is now the possession of the boss. All gang-related scenarios touch on this theme, as do historic tales of kings and their followers, who may change sides and then need to come back into the fold. In all cases tension

is created by the lack of trust that may now ensue
between the various parties.

(5) One member of a marriage begs forgiveness. A
husband or wife has committed adultery. The affair
ends and the supplicant begs forgiveness, wishing for
the marriage to continue.

There are a few variations which, in each case, would
alter the psychology of the situation:

(a) A wife discovers her husband's infidelity (or vice
versa). She confronts her husband. His supplication is a
reaction to being exposed as an adulterer.

(b) The wife is unaware of the adultery, but the
husband's guilt forces him to supplicate, to beg her
forgiveness. This is also moderated by whether the
adultery was in the past or more recent.

The wife has choices. To forgive? To end the
marriage? To continue the marriage but not to forgive?
To try to forgive but struggle with the situation?

Again, the crucial question is where the scene occurs
within the narrative. If it is near the beginning, then
the drama centres on whether the wife can ultimately
forgive and the marriage recover. If it is near the end,
then we have a sense of a kind of cruel punishment
being handed out.

(c) In **Leaving Las Vegas**, Ben is drinking himself to
death but wishes to be forgiven by Sera, a prostitute he
has fallen in love with. There is no sense of punishment
nor any particular future (he is dying), more a spiritual
tidying up of a cruel situation created by him.

2. DELIVERANCE (RESCUE)

DELIVERANCE: *The action of being rescued or set free, saved from something dangerous or unpleasant; prayers for deliverance.*

Synonyms: *redemption, salvation, acquittal.*

EXAMPLE:
It's a Wonderful Life (Frank Capra, 1946)
James Stewart plays a man whose life has fallen apart. As he is about to commit suicide, an angel intervenes and reminds him of all of the great things he has achieved.

Possible Scenarios

The **UNEXPECTED** arrival of a **PROTECTOR**, who comes to the rescue of a **DISTRESSED** character.

Typically, the situation is dire: all hope is gone, all avenues explored and abandoned. The deliverance comes as a surprise (but the seeds must be contained within the script somewhere, otherwise the audience will not buy into it).

EXAMPLE:
A World War II story. The prison of a condemned spy is bombed by the RAF, and in the confusion that follows he escapes. We were not expecting it, but in the context of a world war stranger

```
things have happened, and the audience will
accept this.
```

However, if this device were to be used at the end of a narrative, it would be unsatisfactory. Used earlier, it is acceptable as it allows the story to go somewhere else quickly and we need not ponder on the coincidence for too long. (Also, the film would set up the coincidence through editing.)

In the classic short **An Occurrence at Owl Creek Bridge** (Robert Enrico, 1962), a condemned man is hanged from a bridge. The rope breaks and suddenly he is free, running through an idyllic landscape. In the distance he sees a woman (his wife?) and it seems they will be united. Then, in a dramatic edit, we realise that this was all going through his mind as he was pushed off the bridge in the seconds before his neck broke. **DELIVERANCE** was a device.

In **Leaving Las Vegas**, Sera comes into Ben's life unexpectedly, and we assume that through her love she will stop him drinking. In fact, she doesn't, but her presence gives us hope and takes the film out of a more predictable downward slope.

If we use old theatrical devices, they can seem ironic to a modern audience, perhaps a deliberate device of the filmmaker rather than the domain of the characters themselves. This raises a question: is the character merely a pawn in the narrative or its actual motor? Both are valid journeys, but the film-maker needs to be sure which it is. It is also possible to morph from one direction to the other. I suppose we could call this a postmodern approach, but it is not new: writers have always been fascinated by the relationship between the drama and the dramatic process itself.

As the sophistication of audiences increases through exposure to TV, it becomes more difficult to maintain the traditional status of suspension of disbelief. So the modern dramatist has to make a choice: to stay within the cosy safety of a 19th-century dramatic sensibility (Hollywood, most TV), or to be aware of the unreality of reality and so tap into a much deeper connection with a smaller but more evolved audience.

3. REVENGE FOLLOWING A CRIME

REVENGE: *the action of hurting or harming someone in return for an injury or wrong suffered at their hands; the desire to repay an injury or wrong.*

EXAMPLES:

The Revenant (Alejandro González Iñárritu, 2015)
A fur trapper tracks down the man who has left him for dead and killed his son.

In the Bedroom (Todd Field, 2001)
A young man is murdered by the ex-lover of his girlfriend. His grief-stricken father, frustrated by the impotence of the law, takes matters into his own hands and abducts and then kills the murderer.

Gladiator (Ridley Scott, 2000)
General Maximus is betrayed by Emperor Commodus, who orders the killing of his family. Maximus returns to Rome as a gladiator to seek his revenge.

Revenge seems to be the emotional consequence of many of the dramatic situations.

The 'CRIME' (or event) in this situation is specific to the concept of revenge. It has to be something that has a direct emotional impact on our character, something so strong that it creates an obsessive need for retribution.

IT IS PERSONAL!

Possible Scenarios

(1) The killing/attempted killing of a family member. Or someone who has very close emotional ties with our main character – a friend, a lover. This is straightforward traditional drama. The grief or sense of violation or loss is so strong that the revenge is physical/emotional and has dominance over the character. It causes them to lose control and become temporarily insane – **HOT REVENGE**.

What is essential is the idea of love of family or friend or lover. This situation can be the basis for an entire drama: the crime itself would provide the theme and the **REVENGE** would be the journey of the narrative. The longer it takes to arrive at the revenge, the more time the protagonist would have to become calm again and ponder the meaning of it all, so that by the time the act of revenge is possible, he/she may have arrived at a different mindset – **COLD REVENGE**, although sometimes the protagonist decides not to exact revenge and thus becomes vulnerable.

EXAMPLE:
The man seeking revenge on the killer of his brother then finds he cannot shoot him and walks

```
away, only to get a bullet in the back from the
man whose life he has just spared.
```

If the revenge occurs very soon after the event that caused it, then the protagonist is still possessed by hot revenge and will not hesitate to shoot.

(2) The dishonouring of a female family member.
   (a) The rape of a family member.
   (b) Any kind of sexual contact with a female of the family not sanctioned by the senior male figure (father, elder brother, religious leader), even if the woman was a willing partner.

This opens a debate that reoccurs throughout the 36 situations, so many of which are based upon a theory of male superiority and the idea of drama being about 'what men do' and a domain in which the women cause trouble and then have to be rescued or punished. We need to rethink this notion. It is the duty of the writer to try to avoid gender cliché.

Under the banner of 'honour' a chain of revenge can be set in motion which involves the killing of the male 'criminal', and in many cases the female too, whether compliant or resistant to the crime.

While this scenario is at its most visible within Asian culture, it also exists in Latino settings. But in more subtle forms it is also European/Christian, with its emphasis on Original Sin and the ever-popular idea that it is the woman's fault for being such a temptation (particularly in film noir). We

quickly recognise and buy into this idea because it is so deeply rooted in the politics of Christianity. So, time to move on.

In the 19th century **REVENGE** was the exclusive domain
of the male. In the 21st century it can equally be the female
prerogative: a mother may seek revenge for a crime against
her son.

(3) False accusation.

  (a) The destroying of a reputation by malicious
  gossip. The deliberate spreading of lies. The deliberate
  spreading of a truth that is being hidden in order
  to protect family, etc. (In contemporary drama the
  Internet cannot be excluded from any scenario.)

  (b) False accusation of a crime. Even when proved to
  be false, the damage is done. 'No smoke without fire' –
  reputation and career ruined.

```
EXAMPLE:
The Wrong Man (Alfred Hitchcock, 1956)
A man's life is ruined after he is falsely
accused of a crime.
```

  (c) Loss of property and wealth in absentia. This
  could be a crime by a group or an individual, and such
  a situation would provide the basis for an entire drama
  as the protagonist struggles to retrieve what is rightly
  theirs.

(4) Revenge on an entire gender for the crime of one. The
  extreme example given in Polti's book is that of Jack

the Ripper, on the basis that the killer was revenging himself on womankind because of a crime committed by a single female.

A more subtle illustration would be of someone damaged in a love affair who then blames an entire gender. If it was a man, he would become a misogynist, incapable of loving a woman until (of course) the right woman turns up and unlocks his heart again – in which case the drama is built upon the possibility that he will once again be hurt by love. Typically, he tries hard to find evidence, misreads signals and closes down the emotion, only to discover it was all a mistake. This works just as well if the genders are reversed.

(5) Revenge on an entire race for the crime of one. The basis of all racism. One group looking for a reason to attack another group will seize upon a crime by one person to justify an attack on the larger group. The crime itself may be fabricated and exaggerated in order to justify the bigger action. German fascism was built upon the idea that the Jews were a criminal underclass. All over Europe minority groups are under threat and invariably characterised as criminal.

(6) Revenge via karma. The idea that fate will at some point exact revenge on a person for an unpunished crime (the last scene of **All About Eve** (Joseph L. Mankiewicz, 1950)) – and only the audience will know.

'Revenge is a dish best served cold.' It may be that the act of revenge takes place a long time after the crime – so long, in fact, that the criminal may even have forgotten about it. The revenge is something of an enigma until the motive is finally revealed – a favourite device of many crime writers.

4. REVENGE CONTAINED WITHIN A FAMILY

EXAMPLE:
Festen (Thomas Vinterberg, 1998)
At the 60th birthday party of Helge, a successful
hotelier, his eldest son, Christian, decides to
finally expose his father for sexually abusing
him and his twin sister (who has committed
suicide).

From the beginning of time drama has focused on family. Animals nurture their young and then, at the appropriate time, release them into the wild. Humans do not. We create family tribes. One of the main differences between the theatre of the 19th century and cinema is that the family has changed radically. In a post-industrial culture we no longer need the traditional family structure, but its absence is keenly felt and we have not successfully adjusted to this new reality. As ideas of family still dominate all drama, the absence of family is itself a statement about family. The majority of these 36 situations will, in one way or another, refer to family. We view ourselves on the world stage as a group of families – tribes, races, religious groups – but, sadly, very rarely as one extended family (the family of man).

Families tend to live in close proximity to each other, and in this hothouse emotions can become intense – rivalry, desire, jealousy, ambition. When things are going smoothly a family can be a fortress, a powerful force. But when things start to go wrong the emotions that are released can be vola-tile – the stuff of drama.

In early drama violence within the family was common. Brothers, fathers and sons, fathers and daughters all slaugh-tered each other regularly in the name of a power struggle or split allegiances. In contemporary drama the violence tends more to be of the psychological variety.

INFIDELITY can cause revenge. One partner is unfaithful, and the other takes a slow psychological revenge spanning years.

A son or daughter may take revenge on a parent for a number of reasons. For example, the father is kicked out of the house by the mother, and the children punish her for this.

EXAMPLE:
The Kids Are All Right (Lisa Cholodenko, 2010)
Two children of lesbian parents bring their
biological father into the family environment,
with disastrous results.

5. THE PURSUED – THE FUGITIVE – THE OUTSIDER

PURSUE: *to follow or chase in order to capture or kill.*

Synonyms: *go after, seek, trail, track, hound, hunt down, harass, harry, haunt.*

FUGITIVE: *a person fleeing from hostile parties.*

EXAMPLES:

The Fugitive (John Ford, 1947)
A priest is on the run from revolutionary Latin American militia. He's also having a crisis of faith.

No Country for Old Men (Joel Coen & Ethan Coen, 2007)
A hunter stumbles across a cache of drug money and is pursued by the spirit of retribution.

While pursuit can be a part of many of the other situations, in this category we focus on the isolation of the character being pursued. We are interested in what they are fleeing from, but primarily we focus on the psychology of their journey.

By definition, the protagonist is an outsider, perhaps a social misfit, and usually we are sympathetic to this character. In the creation of dramatic situations a vital element is the audience's ability to empathise with a character, and in the case of the pursued it is easy for an audience to feel the scenario keenly: the absence of friends and comfort; the lack of security and the loneliness. We see the world from the fugitive's point of view. Everything is a potential threat – even the normal can seem ominous – and no one can be trusted entirely. Don Siegel's **Invasion of the Body Snatchers** (1956) is a good example of this.

In a 21st-century scenario we can substitute the word 'outsider' for 'fugitive'. While no one seems to be pursuing him/her, the alienation is the same. In film the exploration of the internal mental world is highly possible.

Possible Scenarios

(1) Fugitive from justice, in which case he/she may be guilty or not guilty. Either way, the forces of law and order will be searching for them. A clock is usually ticking – finding evidence to prove their innocence, the tracking down of the real guilty party, etc. We may also suspect that the state itself is guilty; a dissident fleeing from a totalitarian situation would have our sympathy despite being guilty in the eyes of the state.

(2) Fugitive from love. The protagonist may be in love with a dangerous character and is fleeing from the situation (29 – **AN ENEMY LOVED**).

(3) Hero in exile, but in danger from agents of the state from which he has fled.

(4) Hero regarded as mad or dangerous – as a result of false rumours spread by enemies. Leads to isolation, loneliness, alienation, paranoia.

A paranoiac is a man in possession of the facts.
William Burroughs

What interests us in drama is how the character deals with all of this. In (1) and (3) it is fairly clear-cut: by enduring physical danger and hardship. In the others, it is more psychological. As the situation intensifies, the character has to show great strength of will to survive. We see the psychological damage that it is doing.

Sometimes the fugitive may be offered friendship, but rejects it out of fear and mistrust. A cautious love affair may take place. The power of love (and desire) can occasionally bypass the mistrust temporarily (desire is strong) and cloud the fugitive's judgement, but within this particular genre there is the idea that something negative will come out of desire. This obviously harks back to biblical clichés about how women will always lead men down the wrong road.

```
EXAMPLE:
North by Northwest (Alfred Hitchcock, 1959)
An advertising executive is mistaken for a
government agent by foreign spies. He is aided in
his escape by a glamorous blonde but is not sure
if he can trust her.
```

From a writing point of view this situation is very productive. As it can really focus on the inner workings of a character, it gives us the opportunity to create a tense psychological drama, rather than something inherently plot-driven.

It would seem obvious that the best position for the **PURSUIT** would be in the middle of a story, preceded by the event that causes the fugitive to go on the run, and followed by a resolution of sorts in which justice is finally served and the hero is at last free from pursuit.

A typical cinematic device is the **FLASHBACK**. In the case of the **PURSUIT**, using flashbacks means we can begin the story knowing very little about the protagonist, but then, detail by detail, we can inform the audience of their past – their backstory. In so doing we involve the **ENIGMA** (11) situation and gradually fill in the gaps in the story. The advantage of the flashback is that it is an entirely economical form of storytelling, and it also adds to the tension in a positive way. It is a truth in drama that sometimes the more we know about a character, the less interested we become. Mystery is compelling and causes the audience to begin asking their own questions about the scenario. But we need to pay this off at the right moment.

THE CHASE

The ability of the camera to be in motion during a chase, taking the point of view of both the pursuers and the pursued, engages the audience in a way that is not possible in theatre. Have you ever seen a good (let alone believable) chase on stage? Often the attempt is farcical, and is best used in stage comedy.

EXAMPLE:
The Grand Budapest Hotel (Wes Anderson, 2014)
A hotel concierge is chased across a country by the vengeful relatives of his late mistress.

The cinematic chase is also very useful when it comes to waking up the audience. Say you have two intense, quiet scenes, both vital to the story but lacking in physical energy: a good chase will definitely refresh the air. The problem comes when this device is used to convince the audience that something is happening when actually it is not. The action film can sometimes be described as a series of meaningless chases with some schematic dialogue in between to feed the audience a few road directions.

6. DISASTER

DISASTER: *a sudden accident or a natural catastrophe that causes great damage or loss of life; an event or fact that has unfortunate consequences.*

Synonyms: *calamity, catastrophe, collapse, failure, fiasco, tragedy, misadventure.*

Life is a stage set to be swept away.
J. G. Ballard

EXAMPLES:
Melancholia (Lars von Trier, 2011)
A rogue planet has entered the solar system and is on a collision course with Earth.

Titanic (James Cameron, 1997)
A huge passenger liner collides with an iceberg and sinks.

The exploration of disaster is a fundamental cornerstone of all drama: how it is dealt with; the possibility of recovering from it; its testing of the human spirit and our ability to deal with great suffering and hardship for long periods of time. We are not interested so much in the disaster itself (although this can have exciting screen value) as its after-effects, the converting of chaos back into some semblance of order.

Possible Scenarios

(1) Reversal of fortune. War is often a factor in disaster situations. There have always been wars, and current evidence suggests we are continuing with this way of conflict resolution. And wars will always create disasters.

(2) Defeat. A leader overthrown, invasion by an alien group, loss of wealth, property, possessions or civil rights, humiliation.

This situation also tends to be accompanied by a temporary breakdown in law and order. In the void created as one system is replaced by another, anarchy prevails. There is an absence of the conventional system of protection for the individual. Women become prey to sexual attack, the value of human life decreases.

(3) The loss of loved ones – family members, friends. In any drama that deals with genocide – be it the Jews in Europe in World War II, Rwanda or Bosnia – the same **DISASTER** rules apply.

(4) Natural disasters – earthquakes, floods, fires, tidal waves, etc. Structures and possessions are destroyed in an instant without warning. The only difference between this scenario and war is that the aftermath has less negativity and much more of a focus on restructuring. See, for example, **The Impossible** (J. A. Bayona, 2012), which is about the 2004 Indian Ocean tsunami.

(5) Disasters of love. Although seemingly trivial by comparison to other disaster scenarios, the majority of people in an audience will have experienced the intense

pain and suffering of being rejected in love and will be aware of how this internalised suffering can seem to eclipse all other forms of disaster. Therefore, it is not surprising that this particular situation is so prevalent in drama. It can create behaviour in the victim that is **OBSESSIVE, IRRATIONAL** or **VIOLENT**, which in turn can lead us into many of the other situations.

7. CRUELTY AND MISFORTUNE

CRUELTY: *actions that cause suffering; a desire*
to cause others to suffer.

MISFORTUNE: *adverse fortune; bad luck;*
an unfortunate event.

EXAMPLE:
Son of Saul (László Nemes, 2015)
A Hungarian Jew (Saul) survives in a Nazi con-
centration camp by working in the gas chambers.
He recognises one of the victims as his own
illegitimate son.

Nobody knows you when you're down and out.
That's when you discover who your real friends are.

A key element is that we are almost certainly sympathetic
to the plight of the protagonists, who are innocent of any
crime. It speaks to ideas of injustice, something everyone in
the audience will think they have been the victim of, so they
easily identify with the drama and are prepared to go on the
journey of increased misfortune.

Just when you thought it could get no worse.

There is an element of sadomasochism in all audiences as
they observe the drama of cruelty and misfortune.

There but for the grace of God go I.

It is one of the fundamental situations, and in that respect nothing has changed from the 19th century to now: survival remains a precarious entity.

Possible Scenarios

(1) An innocent person becomes the victim of the ambition of other parties, a disposable pawn used as a device and then sacrificed when no longer useful to the scenario of ambition.

(2) A vulnerable character is protected, sheltered by supposedly friendly people, but is then taken advantage of, assaulted, robbed. It could be a refugee, a woman who is raped by the very soldiers who are protecting her. This brings into play a very dark human characteristic: the ability to lose respect for the vulnerable, the weak, the disadvantaged. It could apply to the deliberate beating up of someone who is homeless, old, mentally ill . . .

(3) A deliberate wounding of the heart.

(4) A desperate person is robbed of all hope, either deliberately or casually.

(5) A loved one loses the affection of a group. This is a complex and interesting category that can be explored from many angles.

All groups are bonded by something – respect, fear, ambition. But in some instances the bond is affection. A group of friends, by definition, would have affection for each other. This builds up over a period of time and within any group may increase or decrease according to the ebb and flow of experiences. In older groups, it tends to be more stable, and it would take a momentous event for the structures of affection to change. But in younger, more volatile groups there is more danger of this happening. A group of schoolgirls, for instance, has certain characteristics that define it as different from a group of young males. The function of alpha and beta is a crucial dynamic, and this shift is being tested all the time in younger groups. A change in the order brought about by the arrival of a new member of the 'gang' can result in another individual being dropped from the group's affections. Similarly, some action of the victim may have triggered their falling out of favour. Malicious gossip and rumours may have created the situation.

Once this situation has been established, we have choices to make within the drama. Do we reveal the reason for the change? If we withhold this information, the victim has to go on a journey to discover the reason, and the journey itself will result in a change in the victim's attitude towards the group. To be dropped from the group forces the victim to become introverted, and it is possible that this introversion may, in the long run, seem preferable to being in a group dynamic that requires constant maintenance. Sometimes it is easier to be on your own, but perhaps this is only discovered once you are dropped by a group. If events then change and the group wishes to welcome back the victim, he/she may decide to stay outside, no longer trusting the dynamic of the group.

EXAMPLE:
The Tribe (Miroslav Slaboshpytsky, 2014)
In a boarding school for deaf children a teenager struggles to fit in.

This scenario also ties in with (1) **SUPPLICATION**: does the victim have to beg for forgiveness in order to be able to regain the affection of the group?

Arguably, it is just as difficult for a loved one to adjust to being unloved as for an unloved one to adjust to being loved.

(6) Through no fault of their own a loved one finds themselves deprived of the love of a husband/wife. The unloved is an innocent.

(7) Deprived of love for a betrayal which the partner cannot forgive.

(8) Unjust punishment. The protagonist is punished for the crime of another. In a war situation, for example, soldiers are attacked by partisans and, in reprisal, innocent civilians are rounded up and punished.

EXAMPLE:
The Ascent (Larisa Shepitko, 1977)
Two Soviet partisans are arrested, along with a group of villagers. They are all hanged.

(9) A sacrifice unnoticed. This is interesting because it raises subtle nuances of behaviour and questions the

nature of sacrifice and selflessness. The person making the sacrifice does so quite deliberately and, therefore, is not really innocent, but it is implied that some kind of acknowledgement or reward will follow. This is possibly thwarted by a third party. Typically, this could be part of a romantic plot whereby a third party takes the credit for a sacrifice and the genuine author cannot state the truth (for whatever complex reason).

The potential psychology of this situation is useful when dealing with concepts of racism, bullying, sexism, homophobia . . . i.e. the more negative aspects of human behaviour which are always present in cultures.

THE KILLING OF AN UNRECOGNISED FAMILY MEMBER

In this situation it is more useful for the drama if the audience knows the connection but the protagonists do not. The psychology ties into the very strong belief we have in family and the importance of keeping the unit whole.

How this situation can exist

(1) Brothers fighting with opposing armies (in a civil war). In their protective armour they cannot recognise each other until after the killing. In this case the audience need not be in on the act; they can discover the tragic result at the same time as the protagonist.

(2) Families split up through civil unrest who have lost contact with each other. They no longer recognise the family connection.

(3) The unrecognised family member is a child born out of marriage, adopted and now with a different name.

In such a case the killer might never know the irony of the situation, but the audience does. The situation can remain enigmatic, which creates an interesting frustration on behalf of the audience, but one should be careful not to overly frustrate them as this can be counterproductive.

(4) The situation can also be used to create tension right up until the last minute, when one of the protagonists recognises something about the other and chooses not to kill (this can tie in with (2) **DELIVERANCE**).

8. REVOLT

REVOLT: *to take violent action against an established government or ruler; to break away from or rise against constituted authority, as by open rebellion; cast off allegiance or subjection to those in authority; rebel; mutiny; refuse to acknowledge someone or something as having authority.*

EXAMPLES:

The Battle of Algiers (Gillo Pontecorvo, 1966)
The Algerian war of independence seen from the guerrillas' point of view.

On the Waterfront (Elia Kazan, 1954)
A dock worker (Marlon Brando) becomes politicised when he observes the injustice and corruption of the union, and refuses to toe the line despite being aware of the brutal consequences of his actions.

Spartacus (Stanley Kubrick, 1960)
Spartacus leads the slaves in a revolt against the Romans.

REVOLT focuses on the relationship between:
(a) oppressor and oppressed;
(b) the tyrant and the victim;
(c) the powerful and the weak.
It is usually (but not exclusively) the stuff of political drama.

Possible Scenarios

The richer, stronger, power-wielding ruling class or aris-
tocracy exploit and dehumanise the peasant and working
class, who grumble and complain about their lot but lack the
strength, courage and organisation to confront their oppressors. Attempts have been made in the past but these have
failed and have been punished by further hardships, which
further foment the appetite for **REVOLT** in a vicious circle
of misery. The oppressors realise this and try to single out
potential troublemakers and eradicate them.

Within this miserable scenario, a heroic leader has to
emerge. At first he cannot gather support, as people are too
intimidated and frightened of what might happen to them.
So he must win them over by a very public act of outstand-
ing bravery. This results in the gathering of a small group of
followers, brave, but not quite as brave (or smart) as the hero.
The hero is without doubt an alpha figure. This is not a co-
operative venture; it requires a leader who gathers disciples.

This small group begins the process and then others follow,
the momentum increases, and finally we have a **REVOLUTION**.

```
EXAMPLE:
V for Vendetta (James McTeigue, 2005)
'V', a shadowy freedom fighter, plots the over-
throw of an authoritarian government.
```

VARIATIONS

(1) In a larger context, one leader may influence other
    leaders to unite against a common enemy, as in the
    Star Wars films.

(2) A factory worker, seeking to improve working conditions, may try to form a union in order to take on the bosses. In 20th-century dramas this was a common theme used by writers such as John Steinbeck. In a film like **On the Waterfront** this idea is reversed and one man takes on the unions (who have become corrupt) in order to improve the lot of the workers.

(3) The whistle-blower. This character is often castigated by his peers for spoiling the system. Everyone recognises the innate corruption; however, they are earning good money. The whistle-blower has a crisis of conscience and, despite knowing that their actions will not be applauded by their peers, decides to spill the beans to the press. He/she can only expect anger and dismay as a result. But the action is morally based and for the greater good of the community. With the proliferation of the Internet this will always be a hot topic (WikiLeaks, Edward Snowden et al.)

EXAMPLE:
The Insider (Michael Mann, 1999)
A research chemist decides to expose the harmful effects of cigarette smoking.

REVOLT is often firmly rooted in some kind of political context and raises the Marxist idea that 'Power corrupts, absolute power corrupts absolutely'.

The protagonist has to have strong characteristics – courage, perseverance, endurance in the quest for truth – but must also be prepared to face ejection from social circles and the loss of friendships, etc. As the tide begins to turn and people slowly realise the truth and recognise the courage of the protagonist, then he/she may be invited to rejoin the old groups, but by now our hero may have recognised certain truths about group behaviour and can no longer be the same person as before.

Was it worth it?

They see the shallowness of the very people they were trying to help.

We may choose for the hero to be thwarted, not quite succeeding in their quest but leaving a strong message for the next wave of revolution. Che Guevara failed in Latin America but became a huge figurehead for the generations that followed.

EXAMPLE:
Battleship Potemkin (Sergei Eisenstein, 1925)
Low-ranking sailors in the Russian navy revolt against their officers over the appalling conditions that they have to endure.

Let us think about the context of **REVOLT**. Is it the big picture or the small one? Are we following the protagonist, is the drama from their point of view? Or are we observing the conflict from a much more detached viewpoint, seeing the machinations of conflict almost like a documentary, where each move and counter-move is given equal weight? Obviously, in a drama the plot and counter-plot are important, and by combining elements of each approach we can show the size of the struggle, at the same time putting the audience's sympathies with the struggling characters. It would be most

unusual to have the audience sympathise with the bosses, but
not out of the question.

PSYCHOLOGICAL REVOLT
A character may revolt against another person or group with
no thought of converting anyone to his/her cause. This is a
psychological drama played out in a very lonely environment.

(1) A prisoner undergoes all kinds of deprivations and
    mental torture. They are determined not to go under
    and to maintain personal dignity and identity.

    EXAMPLES:
    Cool Hand Luke (Stuart Rosenberg, 1967)
    A prisoner refuses to be cowed by the jail
    authorities.

    The Hill (Sidney Lumet, 1965)
    Military prisoners in a British desert camp come
    into conflict with a sadistic officer who is
    determined to break their spirits.

(2) A patient is wrongly incarcerated in a mental hospital,
    a psychological version of being buried alive. We know
    they are not insane. **One Flew Over the Cuckoo's Nest**
    (Miloš Forman, 1975) is a good example. At some point
    the hero has to pretend to be mad in order to survive
    the brutality of the regime. He/she then becomes
    convinced that most of the patients are not actually
    mentally ill and begins organising them, encouraging
    them to voice their opinions, etc. This creates a small

war with the powers that be. It is quite rare for these
scenarios to have optimistic resolutions. The mental
hospital has always been a metaphor for the bigger
society, raising interesting issues about the meaning of
'normal' and 'mad'.

9. DARING ENTERPRISE – BRAVE ADVENTURE

ENTERPRISE: *a project or undertaking, especially a bold or complex one.*

EXAMPLE:
Apollo 13 (Ron Howard, 1995)
A moon mission goes wrong when an oxygen tank explodes. The mission is aborted and the crew have to overcome huge obstacles in order to make it back to Earth alive.

A problem presents itself, and it seems almost impossible to rectify.

Houston, we have a problem.

Someone comes up with a plan (involving themselves as problem solver) that just might work. A hero? A fool? Someone with little to lose? **The Martian** (Ridley Scott, 2015) is a good example of this kind of situation.

The plan is evaluated, and the general consensus is that it has a very small chance of succeeding. The audience is made aware of various possibilities:

(a) many things can go wrong;

(b) luck is an element, and that is out of everyone's control;

(c) the risks are high, loss of life a distinct possibility;

(d) even if the mission succeeds, there is no guarantee

that the 'hero' will make it back alive;

(e) if it is a war situation, it is often made clear to the hero that if they are captured, they are 'on their own'. The mission is not officially sanctioned.

The audience can enjoy the fact that the odds are heavily stacked against the protagonist. Obstacles have to be overcome one by one, each progressively more difficult.

```
EXAMPLE:
Argo (Ben Affleck, 2012)
A man posing as a Hollywood producer tries to
rescue six Americans trapped in Iran.
```

KEY ELEMENTS: bravery, sacrifice, honour.

> *It is a far, far better thing that I do now.*
> *A Tale of Two Cities*

Often the protagonist is something of an outsider with less to lose than others. He/she could be unpopular, previously a coward, and the mission offers a chance of **REDEMPTION**.

Possible Scenarios

(1) **DARING ENTERPRISE** works well in the context of men and war. War stories are inevitably built around the idea of military problems that have to be solved and men and women being constantly tested for courage and honour.

(2) The ticking clock: something has to be achieved within a set time, otherwise worse things will happen.

(3) The courage of one person, or a small group of heroes.

(4) The taking of risks, unselfishly, the protagonists united by loyalty and a common purpose.

```
EXAMPLE:
Saving Private Ryan (Steven Spielberg, 1998)
A group of soldiers go behind enemy lines to
rescue a comrade whose brothers have been killed
in action.
```

Of course, in other films, like the **The Magnificent Seven** (John Sturges, 1960) and **The Dirty Dozen** (Robert Aldrich, 1967), we start with a variation. A group of tough guys get involved in a mission for which they have no loyalty; they are, in fact, mercenaries, but events force them to humanise, and in the end they become honourable. Some of them have to be sacrificed – possibly characters who have already become honourable – in order to convert the others. By the end of the drama they have arrived at a less cynical point of view.

In some contemporary horror genres the concept of daring adventure has mutated and the protagonists are portrayed as being capable of resorting to the most base behaviour in order to save their own lives (e.g. the **Saw** franchise). Again, this is a gender cliché that needs a rethink.

Daring Enterprise – Love

```
EXAMPLES:
The Story of Adele H. (François Truffaut, 1975)
```

A young woman (Victor Hugo's daughter) falls in
love with a British cavalry officer, who spurns her
after their affair. She sacrifices everything for
love and follows him around the world in an attempt
to win back his affection. Her adventure fails.

The Graduate (Mike Nichols, 1967)
A young man falls in love, ruins the relationship
by having an affair with the mother of his love,
and then has to overcome every obstacle in order
to win her back.

This is traditionally a male-dominated genre. The hero is
often seen as out of his depth and from a different class than
the woman he admires. Her family probably disapprove of
him and create barriers to the relationship – at which point
the adventure begins. Try reversing the gender.

Perseverance is the key element here. Sometimes the hero
gives up, exhausted. Everything has failed, the object of affection has not responded, but we, the audience, know something he does not: that she has begun to see his attractive
side. But he took the decision to give up the quest because he
was not aware of this.

Now, at last, the female can be proactive rather than reac-
tive, but first she has to make a decision which would involve
a radical change in behaviour.

By now the audience is completely engaged. Everyone
understands the situation – the difficulty of coming off one
course of action and beginning a new one. Pride, stubborn-
ness and timing become vital elements. Of course, the audience knows that 99 per cent of the time things are going to

work out fine, but the drama can play on the uncertainty of the moments.

He is walking away. Up until now she has been rude, rejecting, disdainful of his advances. He came to say good-bye and she tried to be more open, but he was so caught up in his own pain that he failed to see the signals. She has a very small amount of time in which to stop him. She takes a deep breath, makes a decision and is about to stop him when another event gets in the way and he drives off in his car.

As with all of the situations, what is vital is where in the narrative this scenario belongs. If it is at the end of the story, then some kind of resolution is called for:

(a) the lovers are finally joined together;

(b) she does not move in time and we have a sad ending.

If it occurs in the middle of the story, then we know that there is quite a journey to undertake as the protagonist slowly realises the truth of their love and finds a way to resolve it. Often writers use this as a basis for a tragedy: by the time love is recognised, one of the couple is ill or married to someone else.

10. ABDUCTION

ABDUCTION: *the action of forcibly taking someone away against their will.*

EXAMPLE:
Fargo (Joel and Ethan Coen, 1996)
A businessman arranges for his wife to be kidnapped and held to ransom to solve his financial problems.

Polti's 19th-century book focuses mainly on women as the abducted, and as such it invariably falls to the man to respond, recapture the woman and then possibly take revenge on the abductors in order to save the woman's honour.

Much of this concept remains in contemporary cinema, often taken to new heights of horror and brutality. Women are raped, mutilated and tortured with stunning regularity in various film genres. Men step in and solve the crime, find the perpetrators and deal out justice. There are exceptions (e.g. **The Silence of the Lambs**), but for the most part we continue with this situation and the genre remains male-dominated, tying in with all the biblical stereotypes about gender and sexuality.

EXAMPLE:
The Silence of the Lambs (Jonathan Demme, 1991)
A female FBI agent tracks down a serial killer who abducts and skins his female victims.

In Polti's book the categories were:

(a) abduction of an unwilling woman;

(b) abduction of a willing woman;

(c) the rescue of an abducted woman, followed by the killing (or sparing) of the abductor.

In early pre-cinema drama these situations would have been part of a larger social context – a war, for example, a conflict between two or more rival groups, the idea of a hostage to bargain with. But cinema, with its use of the close-up, immediately began to exploit the intimacy of this situation, the sexual charge of the dominant male and the female prisoner, the potential for complex emotions and danger.

In contemporary cinema we have a choice as to how to deal with **ABDUCTION** and the gender issues that are inherent within these situations:

(a) with restraint, while at the same time acknowledging the intimacy and eroticism of the situation;

(b) exploiting the baser instinct and allowing the male to capitalise on his power. Sadly, an excessive number of films choose this second route and the lines between pornography and exploitation become extremely blurred.

PORNOGRAPHY

This raises important questions about who is controlling and influencing the way in which we make films. Following the film industry's transition from celluloid to digital, it is now very simple and relatively cheap to make a film, and the influence of the porn genre is very clear. Within extreme porn, the concept of **ABDUCTION** is a dominant theme. It is no longer possible to discuss cinema without including porn as part of the equation. Male attitudes towards women (and vice versa) are tied into the sex-film industry, and these values have become assimilated into the mainstream. As film-makers we have a responsibility to be aware of this when we deal with volatile situations like **ABDUCTION**. Clearly, it is a useful device within storytelling: it motivates action and creates drama that everyone can relate to.

11. THE ENIGMA

ENIGMA: a person or thing that is mysterious
or difficult to understand.

EXAMPLES:

Citizen Kane (Orson Welles, 1941)
Kane's last word is 'Rosebud' and a reporter,
Thompson, struggles to see if it can somehow
explain the enigma at the heart of the tycoon.
In the final moments of the film we see that it
is the name of Kane's childhood sledge, which is
tossed onto a bonfire along with other junk.

Ex Machina (Alex Garland, 2015)
A young computer geek finds himself in a lab
where AI machines are being created by an
eccentric genius. Determining what is real (i.e.
human) and unreal (robot) is the enigma before
him. As it deepens, he loses perspective and even
suspects that he himself is a robot.

An **ENIGMA** is an inexplicable situation or event, and in drama
it is useful as a device with which to engage the audience so
that they become involved in the solving of the puzzle.

Arguably, all plots are enigmatic. Information is deliberately withheld from the audience as a means of engaging
their attention. People reading a good script often refer to

it as a 'page-turner', meaning they want to find out what happens next. Therefore, it is a given that all drama is in some way based on **ENIGMA**.

EXAMPLE:

The Marquise of O (Eric Rohmer, 1976)
During a siege a young widow is saved by an
officer. But then, while asleep, she is impreg-
nated. Unaware of this, she later discovers she
is pregnant. Her family turn against her and she
is determined to find out who the father is. The
enigma is finally solved at the end of the film.

When I write a screenplay, I find it useful to have a situation that I myself do not understand. I read newspapers avidly, following crimes and court cases. For example, a defendant may plead innocence of the crime they are accused of. The prosecution may be smarter than the defence team. The evidence may seem ambiguous but by the end of the trial some conclusion has to be reached and the prisoner is found guilty. He/she continues to plead innocence, and maybe twenty years later the conviction is overturned because of new evidence.

EXAMPLE:

Making a Murderer (Netflix documentary, 2015)

Alternatively, the accused is found not guilty, but we all believe this was a result of a technicality and he/she is really not so innocent. What all this boils down to is . . . a **MATTER OF OPINION**.

```
EXAMPLE:
Twelve Angry Men (Sidney Lumet, 1957)
A lone juror convinces the rest of the jury of
the innocence of the defendant.
```

In many instances, without the indisputable evidence of a number of witnesses, plus DNA, plus a confession, it remains a **MATTER OF OPINION**. In fact, there are writers who would love nothing better than to begin a story with this irrefutable evidence and then show that the opposite is true (Sherlock Holmes stories, for instance, use this conceit).

Personally, I care less about the truth or untruth of the enigmatic situation and more about the turmoil and drama that the situation creates within the various protagonists.

For the purposes of this book, what is of interest is how the **ENIGMA** can be used as a plot device. After a choice is made, the situation quickly links itself to a wide selection of other dramatic situations.

The solving of the **ENIGMA** (puzzle) can relate directly to:

(a) saving the life of another person, who may be kidnapped and is possibly scheduled to die on a certain day;

(b) saving one's own life. Again there is the 'ticking clock' theme – the water is rising, the locked door has a combination that must be cracked . . .

Often the solving of the **ENIGMA** can be a life-changing experience for the protagonists, one that leads them to a better understanding of themselves. This could be the point of using **ENIGMA** as a device: for example, a selfish, thoughtless character wrapped up in their own internal world has to deal with a problem and comes to a better understanding of the bigger picture.

Possible Scenarios

SCIENTIFIC VERSUS RELIGIOUS ENIGMAS
(1) To find the cure for a deadly disease.

> EXAMPLE:
> Lorenzo's Oil (George Miller, 1992)
> When his son develops a rare disease, the father decides to find a cure for it.

(2) To conquer the hitherto unconquerable – space flight, undersea exploration, etc.
(3) The meaning of life, does God exist, is there an afterlife, etc.

FAMILY ENIGMAS
(1) What dark secrets can the past reveal? The sins of the father/mother come back to haunt the children.
(2) A love affair in the past is revealed in the present, possibly affecting the children and maybe even causing a dispute about the identity of the true parent.
(3) A traumatic event in the family, a sudden death, and then new information emerges that confounds all ideas of who the dead person really was. In the Italian film **The Great Beauty** (Paolo Sorrentino, 2013) a wife dies. The husband reads her diary and discovers that for all their marriage she has remained in love with another man.

An important element of the **ENIGMA** situation is the notion that we have to constantly adjust our perceptions of people and situations based on new information. Often a story may begin in a conventional manner, and then one small fact will come to light that seems to contradict the existing information. Either the new fact or the body of existing information is wrong. As a basis for a plot, this is good stuff. In an attempt to uncover the truth, the protagonists may come up against resistance, which further solidifies the idea that something is hidden. The audience will always engage with the journey. After all, we all have secrets.

WARNING: when using the **ENIGMA** device there is a danger that the revelation of the enigma will disappoint the audience and then damage the narrative, so great care has to be taken.

12. OBTAINING

OBTAIN: *to get, acquire or secure (something).*

EXAMPLES:
All About Eve (Joseph L. Mankiewicz, 1950)
Aspiring actress Eve Harrington inserts herself
into the lives of a successful theatre clique and
claws her way to the top of the ladder.

Wall Street (Oliver Stone, 1987)
A young stockbroker is willing to do anything to
get to the top.

This scenario relates to the need to get something, implying that there is an obstacle that must be surmounted. Therefore, special means are required to achieve this. The obstacle is not an enigma but something tangible. It is probably out of the range of the protagonist, and in order to 'obtain' it, unconventional methods may have to be used. In this sense it is very different from **AMBITION** (30).

Possible Scenarios

(1) It may be bought, but first the money must be found, which, in turn, may involve:
(a) borrowing it;
(b) stealing it;

(c) selling something of great personal value.
Therefore, delicate decisions and valuations need to be
made.

```
EXAMPLE:
Dog Day Afternoon (Sidney Lumet, 1975)
A man attempts to rob a bank to pay for a sex
change for his lover. When things go wrong, a
hostage situation results.
```

(2) It can be obtained by trickery, by conning someone
with false claims. Eloquence and smooth talking are
required.
(3) Obtaining it using superior force.
(4) Arbitration. Other parties intervene to arrive at an
impartial solution that both parties have to agree on. Art
looted by the Nazis is discovered in a gallery. The children
of the original owners want it back, so a court has to
intervene and make a decision about legal ownership.
(5) Feigned madness. If the objective is to be released
from a situation (military service, an undesirable
relationship, etc.), the protagonist pretends to be insane
or extremely extrovert.

If the 'thing' that needs to be obtained is more abstract –
power, wealth or the need to pass an exam – then the protagonist will need to make more long-term decisions that will
affect them in the future.

(6) Sex: seduction as a career move or to obtain money or
information.

(7) Marriage to someone of power or wealth in order to move to a higher social group. Arguably this is common to all relationships; we only notice it when the difference between the two parties is extreme.

(8) A student from a poor environment may take years to climb the ladder of success, and during that time will observe others succeeding more quickly and become disheartened. Temptations present themselves: short-cut cheating, sexual favours that would speed the process. Moral decisions need to be made, there are pressures from family, etc. A story of struggle and resolve.

(9) The physical struggle, after an illness or accident, to obtain the levels of fitness that existed before.

13. ENMITY OF KINSMEN – FAMILY AT WAR

ENMITY: *a state or feeling of active opposition or hostility.*

It's a family affair.

EXAMPLES:
Force Majeure (Ruben Östlund, 2014)
A husband and wife battle each other over the
truth of what happened during an avalanche.

Long Day's Journey into Night (Sidney Lumet, 1962)
The Tyrone family are reunited after the mother
is released from hospital (after being treated
for morphine addiction). As the story progresses
we see how each member of the family harbours
animosity towards the other.

Some of the most powerful human emotions emanate from
within the family. The claustrophobia resulting from close
proximity, financial issues, sibling rivalry and conflicts of
interest all contribute towards intense drama.

Arguably, the social structures of the 20th and 21st cen-
turies radically changed the physical scenario of family. In
Western cultures it is becoming less common for three or
even two generations of a family to be living together. Afflu-
ence has meant that the economic necessities that once bound
the generations are no longer a factor. The disintegration of

the traditional family and the increase in the ageing population have given rise to new variations on the themes of kin-
ship. Films like **Amour** (Michael Haneke, 2012) have started
to deal with these issues.

FAMILY RIVALRIES/TENSIONS
  (1) Husband–wife
  (2) Father–son
  (3) Father–daughter
  (4) Mother–son
  (5) Mother–daughter
  (6) Brother–sister

These situations are compounded by the fact that all families
are the consequence of a union between two families (and so
on), and the separate families may have very different ambitions. While this was more obvious in previous generations,
to an extent marriage still contains these elements. Each
potential marriage/union represents a possible threat to the
status quo, and the early stages of any marriage can be seen
as the ability (or inability) to fit in within an often inflexible
structure. Throw in elements of religion, class, wealth and
politics, and already there is a loaded situation.

The environment is another factor. Is the family living
within its own ethnic community? If not, is the environment
hostile? A hostile environment increases the internal pressure within a family; a friendly one decreases it but can also
create tension if, for example, the children move too far from
the family's culture.

EXAMPLES:
An Asian family living in the UK. The parents
were raised elsewhere but the children are born
and educated in the UK. The kids' view of their
environment will be radically different from
that of their parents. Also, their attitudes to
religion and morality will be very different.
This will invariably lead to conflicts within
the family, particularly with the father, who
is the automatic head of the family. The mother
will usually have no choice but to agree with
him in any conflict, and the results can often be
murderous.

Catch Me Daddy (Daniel Wolfe, 2014)
A young Asian woman is on the run from thugs
hired by her father.

The more alienated from the wider culture the family is,
the greater the connection within the family. This can lead
to a sense of separation from the environment within which
they exist, which in turn puts huge pressure on the family
itself.

14. RIVALRY OF KINSMAN

Contains strong elements: obsession, eroticism, jealousy,
loss of control, confusion of loyalty.

EXAMPLE:
Written on the Wind (Douglas Sirk, 1956)
Rivalries cause the members of a rich Texan oil
family to tear each other apart, ending in the
death of the eldest son.

What separates this from situation 13 is the influence of
external factors, and how this can escalate the drama to a
higher level of intensity.

Outside circumstances can radically alter the balance of a
family unit: a shift in wealth brought about by the introduction of a new wife or husband, for example. Add to this a possible variation in ethnicity and/or religion, and the situation
immediately becomes charged. The newly introduced person
(through marriage) may have a radically different gender
sensibility, with women being treated as lower beings than
males, etc.

Siblings are programmed to be competitive, and this can
often turn from being healthy to unhealthy, particularly
when, as adults, one of them is markedly more successful
than the other.

The other key area for rivalry within family is through
love and desire.

Possible Scenarios

(1) Two brothers, rivalry for the same woman.

(2) Two sisters, rivalry for the same man.

(3) Brother–sister, rivalry for the same man/woman.

(4) Father–son, rivalry for the same woman – possibly the father's mistress or second wife, or the lover/wife of the son (e.g. **Damage** (Louis Malle, 1992)).

(5) Mother–daughter, rivalry for the same man.

15. MURDEROUS ADULTERY – CRIMES OF PASSION

EXAMPLES:

La Femme infidèle (Claude Chabrol, 1969) (remade as **Unfaithful** (Adrian Lyne, 2002))
The husband seeks out his wife's lover, curious to see what he is like. They meet and it seems friendly, but something the lover says incites an uncontrollable rage in the husband and he murders him.

The Postman Always Rings Twice (Bob Rafelson, 1981)
A married woman plots with her lover to murder the husband.

Body Heat (Lawrence Kasdan, 1981)
A married woman seduces a man she meets in a bar and then convinces him to murder her husband. Too late he realises that he has been used by her and is arrested for the crime, while she walks free.

This situation sits comfortably within the sequence that begins with situation 13, and many dramas have been crafted out of this sequence, often with each situation triggering the next.

ADULTERY was treated more seriously in the 19th century: social attitudes and the legal system lent it gravitas, and gender politics meant that men could treat women as possessions. Any period drama, therefore, can exploit these social conditions to the maximum and the audience will understand the psychology. Contemporary drama continues to be fascinated by this situation. Although adultery is no longer such a serious issue and marriage less common, this situation is as potent as ever.

Any relationship which is built upon the idea of intense love and/or desire has the potential to involve obsession, possessiveness, jealousy, paranoia and, ultimately, madness. If we compare **Othello** with Chabrol's **L'Enfer**, we see very similar dramatic devices at work.

Most often there is a sexual element involved. Desire and passion are strong enough elements to override caution, moderation, philosophical understanding. Characters become irrational, headstrong and crazy, all of which is great for drama.

Possible Scenarios

MURDER OF A HUSBAND BY A WIFE

(1) The husband is murdered in order for the lovers to be together. In a period drama this would make sense because divorce is out of the question and there is no other solution.

(2) The husband is murdered by the wife, helped by the lover, in order to access the husband's money either directly or in the form of insurance. In these situations there is often a twist: the wife is merely using the lover and then implicates him in the murder. This is a typical device in film noir, one that reaches its apogee in **Double Indemnity** (Billy Wilder, 1947) and **The Postman Always Rings Twice** (Bob Rafelson, 1981).

(3) The wife murders the husband because she has discovered his adultery. This murder can be slow and pre-planned so that it seems natural or an accident, or it can be an act of blind rage, a 'crime of passion'.

MURDER OF THE WIFE BY A HUSBAND

It would be an oversimplification to say that the exact same rules apply to a husband. Gender politics remain an unequal affair. Men are usually bigger and stronger than women, and within the hearts of most men there still remains the idea that they have some kind of 'ownership' of the wife or lover. So, while the categories are similar, the psychology is different.

THE MURDER OF A LOVER

Perpetrated by the betrayed husband or wife. The murder can be committed in a fit of passion (as in Chabrol's **La femme infidèle**); another possibility is that the lover has become too possessive and the affair is over for the married person. The lover is now a threat to the security of the marriage and is therefore murdered (as is the case in **Fatal Attraction** (Adrian Lyne, 1987)).

An element to take into consideration: is the lover known to the betrayed party? In Pinter's **Betrayal** (David Jones, 1983), the lover (Jeremy Irons) is the best friend of the husband (Ben Kingsley).

MURDEROUS ADULTERY is fuelled by a heady mix of passion, greed, ambition, eroticism and seduction, all of which are useful dramatic components.

16. ALTERED STATES – MADNESS

MADNESS: *a condition which causes serious disorder in a person's behaviour or thinking.*

Synonyms: *folly, insanity, lunacy, idiocy, foolhardiness, irrationality.*

EXAMPLES:

Repulsion (Roman Polanski, 1965)
A shy young French woman living in London with her more outgoing sister is left alone for a weekend in a gloomy apartment. We see her grasp on reality quickly diminishing.

Black Swan (Darren Aronofsky, 2010)
A young dancer loses her grasp on reality as she is torn between the vicious ambition of the ballet company and her overly controlling mother.

A Woman Under the Influence (John Cassavetes, 1974)
The wife of a construction worker has a breakdown in lonely suburbia.

L'Enfer (Claude Chabrol, 1994)
An obsessively jealous and controlling husband immediately suspects that his beautiful and gregarious young wife is being unfaithful. He begins spying on her, and the evidence further

convinces him that he is right. He begins to lose
his grip on reality.

The 19th-century idea of 'dramatic' madness was a psychological state arrived at as a result of one or more of the
other dramatic situations. The protagonist is driven mad by
an obsession or a series of tragedies that finally unhinge the
victim. Also religious ideas about demonic possession and, in
the case of **Dr Jekyll and Mr Hyde**, the convenience of two
opposing characters residing in the same body.

The dramatic tradition has always used a system of building blocks to tell stories in a structured manner, structures
that are the consequence of logic, cause and effect, action followed by reaction, etc., etc.

Pure madness exists in a void. Actions defy logic and do
not fall into generic patterns. We will come back to this issue
but, in the meantime, let us look at what I will call **DRAMATIC
MADNESS**.

It would be rare to begin a drama with **DRAMATIC MAD-
NESS**, but if we did, we would owe the audience a series of
flashbacks to explain the state of mind of the protagonist. We
meet a character who is catatonic, living alone in a remote
location – an **ENIGMA**? The drama then becomes a kind of
detective story to explain the situation.

When I was in my early 20s, I toured Europe
with a performance-art group. In Belgium we were
approached by a theatre technician who asked a
big favour of us. A friend (English) had been
forcibly committed to a mental hospital and was
in a bad way. Could we go and see him and try to

contact his family, etc.? Reluctantly, we gave
up our Sunday to travel by bus many miles into
the countryside and finally to a grim Victorian
institution. Doors were unlocked, corridors (full
of seriously deranged patients) led to more doors
being unlocked, and then finally we were taken
to a padded cell. The door was opened to reveal
a man with a shaved head in a corner of the room,
his back to us. We walked in, me and my fellow
artists Mark and Laura. After some time the man
turned and stared at us. Then he spoke . . .

'Hello, Mark, how are you?'

Mark looked more carefully. Finally, a
realisation. 'Hey ____, how are you doing?'

By coincidence they had gone to school
together. The guy didn't seem remotely surprised
to see Mark, which made the situation even
creepier. How had he got here? What had caused
his mind to be in this state?

The truth was simple: he'd taken too much acid,
something not uncommon at the time. But as a
writer I immediately began inventing scenarios.
A bad drug experience somehow seemed dull. In
truth, I was disappointed at the lack of a better
dramatic context to frame this amazing, chilly
moment of recognition.

THEATRICAL MADNESS is arrived at after a momentous
shock (or series of them) 'unhinges' the protagonist (often
temporarily). Under this cloak of 'madness' we allow the
subject to behave in ways that would normally not be possible. Madness facilitates the crossing of major psychological

barriers and, most importantly, may engage the sympathy of the audience, particularly if unlawful revenge is the issue. A **CRIME OF PASSION** in French law is seen as more excusable than a premeditated crime, and most legal systems recognise variations on this theme.

Audiences relate to this version of madness, this losing of control. It is a universal theme – we have all said or thought, 'Don't push me, don't push me, I will not be responsible for my actions!' In truth, most of us would not cross that line into loss of control; it would take a series of extreme scenarios to push us. But we recognise the landscape.

Possible Scenarios

(1) Beginning: slowly madness takes over. In **L'Enfer** the newlyweds are happy but the husband demonstrates his potential for jealousy and obsession. Then he begins to imagine that his wife is having an affair. For a moment this is held in check, but then he begins to see clues everywhere. By the end of the film he is insane and a danger to his wife. What is clever about the film is that a great director like Chabrol can present enough of both points of view so that you are not 100 per cent sure if she is telling the truth when she protests her innocence.

When I made **Internal Affairs** (1990), I tried to bring this psychology into the story, so much so that after the first preview the Paramount executives wanted me to make it more explicit that Andy Garcia's wife was innocent of sleeping with Richard Gere. I managed to keep the ambiguity, but many men in the audience still believed she was guilty.

This raises another interesting point. When we write a script, we make choices about what to tell the audience and what to withhold. In most films we are fed all of the salient facts that explain the plot points. It is sometimes interesting to hold back some of this information. This allows the ambiguity to become more potent and the audience to speculate more.

(2) Middle: here madness is a device to move the plot on, to make big changes. The final third of the drama would then deal with the consequences of this madness and the probability that our character regains their sanity. In **Bigger Than Life** (Nicholas Ray, 1956) the main character's growing madness as a side effect of the drug cortisone endangers the lives of his wife and child.

(3) End: madness is the logical conclusion of all that has preceded it, i.e. (6) **DISASTER** and (7) **CRUELTY AND MISFORTUNE**. In **Bullhead** (Michaël R. Roskam, 2011) the main character (played by Matthias Schoenaerts) explodes into madness due to an overdose of the drugs he takes to counter the effect of having his testicles kicked in by a bully when he was a child.

REASONS FOR 'DRAMATIC MADNESS'
A man/woman returns to their village or home and discovers their family murdered, mutilated, raped. Their entire psy-

chological world is destroyed. Their internal logic is useless.
The shock is immense and it unhinges them.

When I lived in LA, I met a man called Bill
Tennant. Bill had been a successful agent and one
of his clients had been Roman Polanski. Polanski
rang him from Europe, worried that he had not
heard from his pregnant wife, Sharon Tate, for
over 24 hours. He asked Bill to go and check the
house. Arriving at the house, Bill was arrested
by the cops who were there in force. Once he
identified himself as a friend, he was led inside
the house and asked to identify the bodies,
victims of the Charles Manson cult. Thereafter
Bill became a drug addict and homeless. When
we met, years later, he was clean and back in
business, and he told me that although he blamed
the incident for his 'madness', he was not sure
now whether it was merely an excuse for other
agendas.

What is interesting for the writer here is that the situation
throws into relief the differences between our internal and
external states – the public face that we present to the world
and our inner being. When things are going well, the two
states are in balance, and we regard this as 'healthy'. But
when extremes begin to separate them, a new tension emerges
that is unpredictable and potentially volatile.

Let us go back to the original scenario. The man/woman
discovers their family murdered, etc. There are two possibilities:

(a) an immediate psychological meltdown. The shock, grief, etc. thrusts the survivor into madness, and at that point anything can happen: a killing spree of revenge on the family of the possible perpetrator of this crime; suicide; a catatonic state and slow death by starvation, etc. Or:

(b) a much slower reaction. At first it seems that the grief is contained, channelled, there's a philosophical acceptance of God's will (or fate). But this is then revealed to be merely the outward presentation of the reaction. The protagonist is able to 'act' normally, but we, the audience, begin to see worrying aspects of their inner state, the slow corrosion of sanity which will ultimately lead to a descent into a much deeper madness.

ISOLATION is a key factor in this dramatic situation. The audience can sympathise with and worry for the protagonist's involuntary journey. We recognise that their communication with other people is no longer genuine, it is acting, and we hope that a character will emerge who can somehow break through the isolation and genuinely communicate with the protagonist, thus halting the descent into madness. But sometimes the situation has gone too far and the protagonist is able to convince the helper that he/she has made contact, merely to neutralise them.

As we begin to deal with issues of real madness, the landscape inevitably becomes darker. I can think of very few mainstream films that deal with pure madness (mental illness) in an engaging way. It is more likely that a drama will focus on characters who have to deal with another character who is mad. But the subject itself is tricky because none of the standard rules of drama (logic, cause and effect) apply within the confines of genuine madness. Also, the universal fear of madness is a factor that makes this, for the most part, a taboo subject.

In **Repulsion** Roman Polanski understands the technique of cinema better than most. Using combinations of sound design, lens choice (the wide angle, the extreme close-up), the acute POV of the subject, camera movement and music, he is able to create a frightening cinematic approximation of psychosis. It is arguable that the power of cinema is such that sometimes one has to hold back its tools because it can become slightly dangerous for an audience.

This is an important point - it is the difference between theatre and cinema. **Repulsion** could only be a film. It could never be that effective on the stage.

Cinema has willingly absorbed all of the elements of surrealism and existentialism, and along with the use of the close-up we have the tools for exploring madness.
   Mike Figgis

THE PSYCHO CHARACTER AND THE PSYCHO CAMERA
Since the beginning of cinema there has been a morbid interest in the psycho. One of the main reasons for this is the abil-

ity of the camera to move and, specifically, the ability of the camera to 'be' a character – one that can hide in dark places, be a voyeur and creep up on unsuspecting victims (usually attractive young women). **Halloween** (John Carpenter, 1978) is a good example of this technique. This is one aspect of cinema that the audience has never become blasé about. Even the most hardened cynic (myself) is still affected by this camera technique, particularly in conjunction with atonal music – a cluster of semitones on the strings over an ominous bass note. It never fails to work. Clearly, it connects with one of the most basic subconscious fears shared by all humanity.

This technique is pure cinema, one that is impossible to achieve in theatre or literature. And it is the technique that is at the core of the 'psycho' genre.

The shower scene in Hitchcock's **Psycho** (1960) is a classic example. Janet Leigh is behind plastic curtains, naked (already Hitchcock was pushing the boundaries of permissive nudity), and the camera is moving. Had the camera been static, locked off, the psychology would have remained neutral, but the fact that it is moving informs us immediately that it is a person, a predator . . . a psycho.

One of the biggest defects of contemporary cinema is a result of the fact that it is now extremely easy to move a camera. They are lighter and equipment is cheaper. Directors confuse the issue, wanting to demonstrate that they can move the camera. It feels very expressive, and as a consequence most TV, cinema, YouTube et al. features a constantly moving camera. By the time we need to utilise the psychology of the camera, its language has become redundant. All is not lost, however: each film is a genre unto itself, and if the camera is disciplined and still, it immediately regains its power.

When thinking about cinema drama and the writing of a script, it is essential to understand these things. After all, if you were writing a piece of music and didn't understand the basic rules of harmony, you would be lost.

In the 'psycho' genre we invariably place the audience on the side of sanity. The cops have to track down the serial killer, who has a complex agenda and a pattern that is mad, one that perhaps only another 'mad' person can understand. In **Manhunter** (Michael Mann, 1986) the character of Will Graham (William Petersen) serves this purpose.

The genre is essentially a variation of **THE ENIGMA**, a complex mystery to be solved.

Arguably, madness in an individual is a matter of opinion. We can all think of examples of characters who were perceived as mad, but in time opinion shifted and they were reclassified as sane.

EXAMPLES:

Invasion of the Body Snatchers (Don Siegel, 1956)
As a small American town is methodically
colonised by aliens who have invaded human
bodies, the one surviving 'clean' human begins to
doubt his own sanity.

One Flew Over the Cuckoo's Nest (Miloš Forman, 1975)
A man is incarcerated in a mental hospital. We
know that he is sane, but the environment makes
it more and more difficult for him to survive.

Forman's film explores several themes of madness: the individual in the context of an institution; how the individual can be rendered insane by being institutionalised. Alternatively, the individual can 'pretend' to be mad in order to achieve something.

Cinema can be a powerful tool for the better, showing the point of view of the person who is thought of as mad. This may show their perception of other people as clearly odd, even psychotic. We see this regularly in films, when the patient seems sane and the doctors and officials odd, distorted and no longer capable of treating the patient as a human being.

In the 1960s the pioneering psychologist R. D. Laing experimented with the treatment of mental illness by making the doctors and staff wear the same type of clothing as the patients.

Cinema is expensive, much more so than theatre, and as such has become aligned to ideas of profit and loss, commercialism, capitalism. It is also the popular culture of our time. It is thought of as an 'entertainment' and 'show business', liberating the stage to deal with weightier issues. There is much snobbery between theatre and film because of the broad range of subjects handled by cinema. Of course, in the pre-cinema days theatre churned out as much crap as film now does, but the fact remains that in order to raise money for a film, many financial bodies have to be persuaded of the commercial prospects of the script. For that fundamental reason it is very rare to find a film that deals with the subject of mental illness.

I attempted it in a small way. **Mr Jones** was a study of bipolar disorder. The studio was horrified by the scenes of depression, the interactions with other psychiatric patients, the grim realities of a state mental hospital. I was ordered to cheer things up, and it was suggested that I incorporate a scene with a hang-glider and a cosy romance with a therapist. More recently, after watching **Silver Linings Playbook** (David O. Russell, 2012), I realised that this was what the studio had wanted: two characters with bipolar disorder looking for the 'silver lining' in their lives.

17. FATAL IMPRUDENCE – THE GAMBLER

IMPRUDENCE: *not showing care for the consequences of an action; rash.*

The element of risk is greater than the chance of success.

Our Father, which art in Heaven, lead us not into temptation!

EXAMPLE:

Fatal Attraction (Adrian Lyne, 1987)
A married businessman gives in to temptation and has a sexual encounter with an attractive woman. Things go badly wrong when it becomes clear that she takes the affair more seriously than he does.

We often portray life as a journey along a road. Back in the 1950s and '60s there was a huge poster in the London Underground for Start-rite children's shoes. It depicted a boy and a girl setting off on the path of life. Continuing the metaphor, a road has many turnings and branches, and **FATAL IMPRU-DENCE** is one of those dramatic

branches: gambling with life, doing something risky, being aware of the consequences but still proceeding. The protagonist is entirely responsible for what may follow and cannot lay the blame elsewhere.

Possible Scenarios

(1) A dilemma exists which cannot be solved by conventional or existing means. The pressure on the protagonist is considerable and their judgement is affected by desperation. But the consequences of failure are visible to the protagonist. An opportunity presents itself and a quick decision is made. There is no premeditation involved. Despite the odds on the possibility of success being so poor, the protagonist takes the plunge. Whether disaster or success follows is the writer's choice, but the scenario has undeniably created dramatic tension and the audience will usually be made to wait for the results to make themselves known.

Example:
Psycho (Alfred Hitchcock, 1960)
A young woman steals money from her office in order to run away with her lover. She regrets it and decides to return the money, but it's too late and things go badly wrong for her.

(2) A happily married man with kids has an affair, not out of unhappiness with his situation but almost out of

boredom. The affair triggers a series of situations that threaten to destroy his life (e.g. **Fatal Attraction** et al.).

(3) A politician begins his life with integrity, proud to represent the people. He works hard for little reward, observes others take bribes and resolves to eradicate corruption. Meanwhile, he struggles to look after a growing family and has many bills to pay. One day an opportunity presents itself: unaccounted money is available, so without letting on to anybody he takes the money, telling himself it is a loan that he will pay back. In fact, no one notices, and he is in such a position of power that he is above suspicion. From this moment on he is compromised. He begins to take the money regularly, now telling himself that he deserves it because he is doing so much good fighting corruption, etc. But now he has to struggle with his own conscience and has become a divided personality. No one ever finds out about the money, but he has corrupted himself.

(4) The act of imprudence can take place within a group. The protagonist is drinking with friends and is encouraged to do something imprudent. Alternatively, they may be trying to discourage the foolish decisions. In the Dutch film **The Loft** (Erik Van Looy, 2008) five friends conspire to conceal the murder of a young woman, who has been found in the loft they share as a place to take their mistresses.

The beauty of this situation is that it introduces the element of **CHANCE** as a major component. An unexpected situation presents itself, and we observe the reaction and wonder how we ourselves would have dealt with the situation.

Note: it is important that the audience is entirely up to speed with what is at stake in this scenario. They need to know what the risk is and invariably take a position on the side of common sense. There will always be the certainty that this will, sooner or later, end badly.

18. COINCIDENCE

COINCIDENCE: *a remarkable concurrence of events or circumstances without apparent causal connection.*

Note: this is a new category, missing from Polti's original, but I feel it is a more essential tool in cinema than it is in theatre.

In music the diminished chord is a useful device that allows the composer to move effortlessly from one key to another without using traditional devices of modulation.

In drama, **COINCIDENCE** allows the dramatist to jump from the linear narrative to a new element without having to use conventional techniques of transition.

```
EXAMPLE:
The Woman Next Door (François Truffaut, 1982)
A young couple buy a house in a small village.
The husband discovers that his ex-lover is their
neighbour.
```

The human race is obsessed and fascinated by the notion of coincidence. It appeals to the idea that there may be a Master Plan after all, a deity out there with control over things (**FATE**).

In drama, we can play the Fate/Coincidence card, but only sparingly. There is an unwritten rule that we must not 'milk' the situation too many times lest we lose the audience's willingness to 'suspend disbelief'.

In order for a coincidence to work well in a story, the elements that are to coincide must be set up thoroughly prior to the event. Using editing techniques, a rhythm needs to be developed that begins to suggest the inevitability of coincidence. This is pure cinema technique, something almost impossible to achieve in live theatre. The cinema audience begins to participate in the inevitability of the situation.

```
The Loss of Sexual Innocence (Mike Figgis, 1999)
A collection of stories built around the myth of
Adam and Eve and their expulsion from the Garden
of Eden. Coincidence played a large part in the
scenario, particularly in the episode 'Twins'.
I introduced adult twins (two women) who'd been
separated at birth. One lives in London, the
other in Rome. The story quickly establishes
that one twin is setting off from London for a
meeting in Rome. Meanwhile, the other is asked to
go to Rome airport to meet a client. In a series
of parallel cuts we bring them ever closer,
right up to the moment when they should meet,
at which point something distracts them and the
opportunity is lost for ever.
```

This was a pure piece of cinema narrative, impossible to tell effectively in theatre or a novel. I was playing with the audience's desire for unity from disunity, subverting the expectation of dramatic coincidence.

The idea of coincidence is universal and, therefore, an

essential dramatic device. Newspapers and TV consistently feature stories built around the theme: family members reunited by coincidence after 60 years; fatal accidents among siblings at the same time on the same stretch of road. We are extremely receptive to the possibility of coincidence and readily accept some bizarre scenarios when presented as fact (often when twins are the subject), which makes this situation a very useful tool in the dramatic structure.

It connects effectively with a number of other dramatic situations:

  (2) **DELIVERANCE**
  (6) **DISASTER**
 (26) **INCEST**
 (27) **DISCOVERY OF THE DISHONOUR OF A LOVED ONE**
 (32) **MISTAKEN JEALOUSY**

Many of these scenarios are arrived at through the use of coincidence: being in the wrong place at the right time; being in the right place at the wrong time . . .

Another interesting variation is the false coincidence: deliberately making a character believe that a remarkable coincidence has taken place, only to discover later that they were set up.

EXAMPLES:
Body Heat (Lawrence Kasdan, 1981)

Notorious (Alfred Hitchcock, 1946)
The daughter of a Nazi sympathiser agrees to try to infiltrate a group of Nazis in Argentina.

In **Notorious** the Ingrid Bergman character is set up to meet the German spy by 'accident' while out riding. In this instance the audience is aware of the set-up. In **Body Heat** (Lawrence Kasdan, 1981) the protagonist is set up by a woman who wants him to kill her husband. His realisation comes too late for him to save himself.

19. DREAM STATE

DREAM: *a series of thoughts, images and sensations occurring in a person's mind during sleep.*

This is another dramatic situation that did not exist in Polti's original.

EXAMPLES:
Un Chien andalou (Luis Buñuel, 1929)
8½ (Federico Fellini, 1963)
Blue Velvet (David Lynch, 1986)

All three of these films have dream-like storylines that are very different from the conventions of linear narrative.

WHAT IS A DREAM?
I would define it like this: it's a story that I tell myself when I am unconscious. I do not know what is going to happen next. Sometimes I am scared, sometimes happy, sometimes aroused. Although the narrative often seems disconnected, I am able to relate to it. Usually the story is incomplete because I wake up, but there is also the sense that the conventions of beginning, middle and end do not apply here. The person who is presenting the story must be 'me' – after all, who else could it be? – but it is a 'me' that I do not know or particularly understand. As long as this relationship remains specific to when I am unconscious it is OK. Were it to cross

over into my waking persona it would be deeply disturbing.

We take our dreams very seriously. They seem to predict things or sometimes warn us, connect us with the dead and allow us to escape the reality of a dull or harsh existence.

Like everyone, I have had many intense dreams, but one in particular had a big impact, and it happened at a time when I was having a series of bad experiences in the Hollywood studio system. I was seriously considering giving up film-making altogether. This was the big question in my mind.

My dream was in 3 equal parts:

PART ONE was a silent film. I do not recall the images, but I remember the absence of sound;

PART TWO was a soundscape, no images at all;

PART THREE was the combination of part one (the film) and **PART TWO** (the sound), which transformed the meaning of both components in a radical way.

I woke with a very clear understanding of what, for me, the power of cinema was, and made a decision to carry on.

PARTICIPATION MYSTIQUE

Carl Jung had an interesting theory about creative fiction and its relationship with an audience. He called it 'participation mystique', and in essence it was this:

A writer or an artist writes something intense and crea-tive, and the reader understands it as if he or she were the actual writer. It's as though the writer has projected all kinds of unconscious material onto the fiction. Jung goes on to say that fiction becomes fact, and that the most bizarre experi-ences can take place within the narrative because the reader is experiencing it directly. There is no need to suspend disbelief because the reader is 'in' the story.

All of which goes some way towards explaining why an audience can be moved to tears by a dramatic tragedy that they know to be fake, to be unreal. Neurologists explain it in a different way: they say that the areas of the brain that deal with emotion respond in the same way to both real and fake signals of tragedy, while other, rational parts of the brain know it to be fake.

André Breton (1896–1966, the founder of the Surrealist movement) suggests that a cinema audience, before being subjugated by a film, goes through a critical stage that is comparable to 'between waking and sleeping'.

The screen itself is an isolated object, seemingly unconnected to its source, whereas in theatre the element of 'flesh and blood' is ever present. Film, projected at 25 frames per second, flickers hypnotically, the cinema environment is dark and cosy, and we surrender to the images on screen. Arguably, the theatre environment has similarly cosy properties, but the resemblance stops there because, as previously discussed, the camera can transport us in a way that mimics the imagination – we can fly. If we compare the use of dreams in theatre with cinema, there is an overwhelming predominance of them in the latter.

What fascinates me about cinematic dream states is this: film is such a powerful medium that it has the capability to change the way we think. It would not be a lie to say that as a result of the language of cinema, people who have grown up after 1930 have a vastly different way of looking at their world than all previous generations. From the beginning of cinema film-makers have been fascinated by dreams; in particular, how they could be visualised by this new and exciting medium.

A few years back I participated in a film/dream project. Forty-two film-makers were each invited to make a 42-second dream film. A very interesting group of artists – including David Lynch, Harmony Korine and Kenneth Anger – participated. The finished films were put together and then projected at the Beijing film museum, and all the participants were invited to the show. The results were diverse and fascinating. It seemed to me that the Chinese film-makers (mostly young and unknown) had opted for humour (I dreamed I won the lottery and kissed a pretty girl, but then I woke up and my wife gave me hell), whereas the Western artists, steeped in the post-Freudian tradition, had gone in various clichéd directions (clocks going backwards, red velvet curtains, dwarves et al.). And it raised in my mind a 'chicken and egg' question: is the way we now dream overly influenced by the way film portrays the dream state? I think the answer is yes, in exactly the same way that our sexuality is now shaped by the cinema experience (influenced by the porn industry).

What are the cinematic techniques that can emulate the dream state?

(1) The jump cut.

(2) The flashback.

(3) Slow motion.

(4) The out-of-body experience – seeing oneself as another person.

(5) A soundtrack that is disconnected from the visual image; or heightened music, in contradiction to the

on-screen images (for example, in **Blue Velvet** David Lynch uses the classic pop song 'Love Letters' as a contradiction to the horrific scene of death that we are watching).

(6) Image-enhancement techniques: monochrome, blur, heightened colour saturation.

EXAMPLES OF CINEMATIC DREAM STATE

David Lynch has a fascination with the dream state, so much so that the word 'Lynchian' has become synonymous with this aspect of film. In a now-famous example from the TV series **Twin Peaks** (1990), Lynch created a unique dream-like atmosphere by tinkering with the very technique of film. First, he filmed the actors doing the scene. He then reversed the film so that the dialogue and moves were all backwards. Next, he gave this reversed footage to the actors and told them to learn the text and moves in reverse. He then filmed them again, this time in reverse mode. Lastly, he reversed the film so that the narrative was now going in the correct direction, except now both the dialogue and the action had a distinctively 'weird' ambience . . . which made it seem very dream-like.

These techniques are beautifully parodied in an indie film:

```
Living in Oblivion (Tom DiCillo, 1995)
The chronicle of a NY 'indie' film production.
```

In one hilarious scene an irate dwarf asks the director why film dream sequences always have to have a dwarf and some dry ice.

THE WAKING DREAM
Much favoured by film-makers (myself included).

EXAMPLE:

An American Werewolf in London (John Landis,
1981)
The protagonist wakes from a frightening dream,
and for a moment all is calm. Then something
happens that is 'dream-like', and with it comes
the realisation that this is merely another phase
of the dream.

20. SELF-SACRIFICE FOR IDEALISM

SELF-SACRIFICE: *the giving up of one's own interests or wishes in order to help others or advance a cause.*

EXAMPLES:
On the Waterfront (Elia Kazan, 1954)
A dock worker (Marlon Brando) becomes politicised when he observes the injustice and corruption of the union, and refuses to toe the line despite being aware of the brutal consequences of his actions.

The Insider (Michael Mann, 1999)
A research chemist decides to expose the harmful effects of cigarette smoking.

Note: both of these examples also use (8) **REVOLT**.

The first of a group of situations to deal with dramatic death, as opposed to death from old age or illness.

Central to this situation is the concept of idealism, the strong belief in a cause, principles, faith. We are dealing with characters who either:

(a) have an unshakeable belief in the idea of a God, one they have held over a long period; or

(b) in the course of the drama have arrived at a belief with the zeal of the convert and are prepared to undergo self-sacrifice for this passionate discovery.

Which gives us two very different psychologies:

(1) A strong character whose beliefs will be put to the
    test in a situation of conflict. For example, a religious
    situation, one belief against another, Catholic versus
    Protestant; or a war situation, where a character is
    captured and tortured to betray his comrades, but is
    ultimately prepared to die for his beliefs. All religious
    histories (the Bible) use this situation. The more
    intense the pain, the more absolute the belief; the
    martyr who dies for the greater good of the people.

(2) A weak character who may have led a life of hedonism
    and waste, but who, later in life, finds something to
    believe in and is prepared to die for this new passion.
    At last their life seems to amount to something of
    value, something 'worth dying for'. Audiences relate
    strongly to these moral examples; they seem to
    illuminate life with a ray of meaning – it is never too
    late to clean up the mess of your life. Thus we often
    create messed-up characters purely so that later we
    can sacrifice them for the greater good of the drama,
    arriving at a kind of redemption. We need to remind
    ourselves constantly that drama is based on a series of
    moral tales, moral dilemmas.

It is also true that audiences like to test themselves through
these situations; they can easily empathise with the conflict
and wonder how they themselves would fare in similar circumstances.

The difference between the two psychological states is
subtle but it allows the writer a choice of where to place the

emphasis. It is a story about the testing of character: will they succeed or fail the test of pain and loss.

What is perhaps more interesting is the character who almost succeeds but, at the last moment, can endure no more and is defeated, and then has to live with this failure. If we start a narrative with this idea, then the story that follows could be about how the character copes with this failure.

```
EXAMPLE:
Silence (Martin Scorsese, 2016)
The Christian religion has been banned in Japan.
A young priest has been sent undercover to
minister to the Christians. He is arrested and
tortured so that he will give up his faith.
```

Inevitably, as storytellers we would want to give the character a second chance, to create another situation in which they are tested again. I do not know of one dramatic scenario in which this second test results in failure. And while the idea of a second failure is almost unthinkable in drama – which is perhaps understandable – it's also unrealistic, as we are constantly confronted by failure after failure in our everyday lives.

LOVE SACRIFICED FOR IDEALISM

The concept of love is a fundamental element in drama. It is a powerful force that can induce madness, irrational impulses, rivalry, jealousy, etc., but it can also lead us to salvation. Therefore, the idea of love sacrificed for an ideal puts it almost on a par with death. In some ways it is even more powerful because it involves another person (the loved one), who will suffer because of this decision, not knowing why they have been cast aside and probably reasoning that it is because of an absence of love on the part of other. In drama we love to torture ourselves with misunderstanding.

This is a much-loved device in romantic fiction.

```
EXAMPLE:
Camille (George Cukor, 1936)
A Parisian courtesan must give up her true love
so that his life will not be contaminated by his
relationship with her.
```

As with all of the situations, the choice of where to place this one is crucial. If we were to place it in the middle of a drama, then we would wait in anticipation for some kind of resolution: the loved one finds out about the sacrifice through a third party or a coincidence and the lovers are finally united, stronger than ever; or he/she finds out, but it is too late and the other has died as a result of the sacrifice.

If we place the situation towards the end of the drama, it has an entirely different result. The audience would sense that it is too late to expect a romantic resolution, that the loved one will not find out about the sacrifice; therefore, the action can be seen as more genuine and less of a dramatic device.

What is interesting here is as much to do with the audience's relationship with the drama as with the devices of the drama itself. We go to a cinema to see a film, knowing that it will be between 90 and 120 minutes long. The placing of specific dramatic situations within that time frame (at the beginning, middle or end) will automatically elicit pre-conditioned responses from the audience, based upon their accumulated memories of the countless films they will have seen. As we create stories we need to constantly ask ourselves, 'What does the audience expect to happen here?' Any good magician will tell you the same thing: 'Appear to give them what they expect and then reveal something new that they did not anticipate.' But always remind yourself that the audience has been here many times before. It is a well-worn path.

CAREER SACRIFICED FOR IDEALISM

Career advancement is synonymous with the concept of understanding rules. Success comes as a result of the ability to use the rules to one's advantage, to anticipate opportunities before they occur, even to create opportunities with the idea of personal success. Large corporations and political parties are based upon these intricate rules, as well as on concepts of loyalty to the body politic.

21. SELF-SACRIFICE FOR FAMILY

Again, as in so many of the 36 situations, we have family as the key dramatic element. There is a universality about family that all audiences understand and can relate to.

But once in a while we encounter a character that seems free of family, and this person can be dangerous in the wider social context because they cannot be manipulated by the conventions of family. After all, most organisations operate as a mirror of family. 'We were like family,' 'He was like a father to me,' 'We were like brothers,' etc. etc. So family is such a big deal that when we come to **SELF-SACRIFICE FOR FAMILY**, we are using big guns. The variations of the situation may already be familiar to many in the audience in as much as they may have speculated as to how they themselves would have behaved had the situation involved them personally. One of the earliest and ongoing functions of drama is to allow the audience to rehearse situations that may occur, as well as those, like death and the loss of loved ones, that definitely will. Technology may be changing the world at an alarming tempo but certain basic family dynamics remain constant.

Possible Scenarios

(1) In extreme situations, war (**DISASTER**). A hostile group invades and takes over the area. New rules are created which immediately threaten the stability of the family. It may be necessary to sacrifice oneself in order to save the life of another family member – a child perhaps. In many war dramas we get a situation where a hostage is taken and used as a bargaining tool, and the protagonist has to give up their life in exchange.

(2) Self-sacrifice for the greater good of the family. An illness is slowing down an escape, creating danger for the family. A sacrifice is necessary.

(3) Sacrifice of personal ambition for the greater good of the family. This is a frequent situation, often involving a father/mother having to choose whether to accept a promotion that will take them away from the family. Often in dramas the decision to take the promotion triggers the idea that this will somehow damage the integrity of the family, that the husband and wife will grow apart, etc. We unconsciously fear this separation in a family. If it is the woman who sacrifices her career, we have to confront gender politics. Sadly, it is far more of an accepted cliché in drama (and in life) that the woman makes this sacrifice. Women are still seen as being the lynchpin for family integrity.

(4) A woman sacrificing her sexuality to protect her family. This is still a taboo in drama but nonetheless a very important subject. A woman is given no choice but to prostitute herself in order to feed and protect

her family. The issue of female honour remains potent in the 21st century. Firstly, the woman has to make the decision to sacrifice herself for the family. Secondly, she often has to deal with the male response to her sacrifice. This may involve a man being unable to come to terms with the situation because the woman is now seen as 'corrupted' by the experience; or the male suffers guilt for not being able to prevent the situation in the first place. It touches on deep questions of gender, possession and power, as do most serious sexual issues.

EXAMPLE:

A Woman in Berlin (Max Färberböck, 2008)
An anonymous female keeps a diary of the Russian occupation of Berlin in 1945. Mass rape takes place and very few women are able to avoid it. There is a kind of solidarity among the women, but the men have great difficulty coming to terms with it.

Further complexities are added to this situation by the factors of timing and visibility. Is the situation known to the wider public within the community? Is it known to the husband? If not, is there a moment in the drama when this skeleton comes of the closet? At this point it would also fall into another category – (27) **DISCOVERY OF THE DISHONOUR OF A LOVED ONE**.

22. EVERYTHING SACRIFICED FOR PASSION (DESIRE – OBSESSION – SEX)

EXAMPLES:

Carol (Todd Haynes, 2015)
A married woman is drawn into an affair with a young female sales assistant. It is set in the 1950s.

Ju Dou (Zhang Yimou, 1990)
A young man falls in love with the wife of his cruel uncle. Their relationship becomes increasingly difficult to maintain, ending tragically.

The Story of Adele H. (François Truffaut, 1975)
A young woman (Victor Hugo's daughter) falls in love with a British cavalry officer, who spurns her after their affair. She sacrifices everything for love and follows him around the world in an attempt to win back his affection. Her adventure fails.

Inherent in this situation is the notion that **SEXUAL DESIRE** is an irrational physical force so powerful that it can overwhelm all that is ordered and rational – a form of madness. As a dramatic idea it is extremely powerful because it immediately connects with all audiences. There cannot be a single person who has not at some time been at the mercy of these emotional forces. Since the beginnings of drama and fiction, passion/desire has been a key element for writers. Is there a difference between theatre and cinema when dealing with this subject?

As soon as cinema was invented, it began focusing on sexuality, and in so doing inhabited the voyeuristic male gaze. It allowed audiences visual access to hitherto private domains of intimacy and secrecy. The English writer Anthony Powell said, 'Never assume to understand the secrets of a marriage' – by which he meant that once the doors are closed, we cannot know the private lives therein. Cinema, however, immediately attempted to breach those walls of privacy. At its crudest, cinema is pornographic, responding to the basest elements of the male domain (and it is fundamentally male), and this has also influenced the way in which it constantly attempts to push its own boundaries with regards to intimacy. Porn is fundamentally concerned with the objectifying of the sexual act, but in drama sex is in itself a dramatic element because it relates characters to each other and creates tension and problems. Drama has little interest in things going well – the perfect relationship that produces perfect children who grow up to become responsible citizens, caring and thoughtful, etc. If I were describing a script with such a situation, the expectation would be for something to go horribly wrong, otherwise why would we care?

Cinema is fundamentally a sensual medium, which often makes it quite dangerous when this power is misused.

We are discussing **EVERYTHING SACRIFICED FOR PASSION**, so we must take a moment to discuss cinematic sex and its complicated relationship with cine drama. It is something that has had a presence in most of the films that I have made. There is no part of the human body left to explore in cinema. What remains as powerful as ever is the interaction between human beings when it comes to love, passion, jealousy, etc. And cinema is the perfect medium with which to handle this complex structure.

SELF-IMPOSED LIMITS

In cinema it is possible to depict almost everything. In theatre it is not, and writers and directors have had to use other devices – visual and verbal – to imply extreme scenarios of sex and death. But it would be a huge mistake to assume that the ability to 'show' something will have the impact the film-maker desires. In the 1960s Jean-Luc Godard stated that it was impossible to show sex and death in cinema. I interpret that to mean that we accept the audience knows that everything in cinema is fake, not real; therefore, the visual impersonation of an extreme act is almost laughable and devoid of emotion – unless it is somehow tied in with strong psychological elements of emotion.

I directed a film version of August Strindberg's play **Miss Julie**. The core of the narrative revolves around a sexual liaison between an aristocratic woman and her servant. In the play, written at the turn of the 20th century, it was not possible to show the sex directly; in fact, even without it, the play was banned in the UK. The work also contains a lot of politics concerning social change in Sweden at that time, information which, for a contemporary audience, is not so interesting. In adapting the text with Helen Cooper, I made a radical choice. I depicted the sex (in split screen) and I moved some of the text from a later scene and used it during the sex. While this annoyed some purists, I felt it was entirely cinematic and appropriate for the film I was making.

When sex is portrayed in cinema, there is a noticeable lack of dialogue, aside from the obligatory moans and groans (I think it was David Lean who asked his actors to imagine they were having an asthma attack), and this seems to me to be a lost opportunity. Given that we can now incorporate sex into a narrative without fearing the police at the door, it is time that we also began exploring the possibilities of sex in directions other than porn.

To come back to the point of this particular situation, when sexual passions are aroused, profound characteristics are changed or amplified, and temporary madness is always an interesting possibility. But it is the responsibility of the film-makers (the directors and writers) to get the balance between the explicit and the evocative right. To be too modest may inhibit the drama, but to be too explicit may constrain the audience's ability to understand the nuances at work.

It is always worth reminding oneself that the visual image easily overwhelms everything else.

Orson Welles said that when you stage a play, each audience member represents a camera, so there are hundreds of cameras all selecting specific visual elements. But in a film there is only one!

Possible Scenarios

(1) A life ruined. Family abandoned. Career halted or finished. Social status ruined. This would apply

particularly to someone in high office who is in
the public eye, someone with clearly defined moral
standards that have to be maintained. Often this places
the protagonist in a vulnerable position for blackmail.

(2) Crossing social barriers. This may involve class,
ethnicity or gender. Until recent times gay love was a
criminal offence (for men but not women) and to be
'outed' often had disastrous results for individuals.

EXAMPLE:
Victim (Basil Dearden, 1961)
A married man is blackmailed because he is gay.

(3) Criminality – crossing legal barriers.
(a) Sex with an underaged person.

EXAMPLE:
Lolita (Stanley Kubrick, 1962)
A middle-aged academic has a relationship with
the underaged daughter of his landlady.

(b) Sex with the enemy.

EXAMPLES:
Hiroshima Mon Amour (Alain Resnais, 1959)
A French woman has a wartime affair with a German
soldier and afterwards is publicly shamed and
humiliated.

Ryan's Daughter (David Lean, 1970)
An Irish girl has an affair with a British

soldier during the Troubles. Afterwards she
suffers at the hands of the mob.

(c) Rape.

EXAMPLE:
Once Upon a Time in America (Sergio Leone, 1984)
The protagonist rapes the woman he is in love
with.

(d) Incest (see situation 26).

POSITION IN THE DRAMA
(1) Beginning: the drama deals with the consequences.
(2) Middle: we see the build-up of the passion and then
how the characters deal with the consequences.
(3) End: we focus on the struggle to deal with the passion,
to contain it. But the passion intensifies and ultimately
the protagonist has no choice but to succumb.

In **The Woman Next Door** (1981) Truffaut neatly uses
all three possibilities. We begin after a passionate affair
has ended. The couple meet again by coincidence, the
affair is rekindled and then contained, but by the end
both characters are lost and die together. Truffaut visits
this scenario again in **The Story of Adele H.**

23. NECESSITY OF SACRIFICING LOVED ONES

EXAMPLE:

Sophie's Choice (Alan Pakula, 1982)
A mother has to make a choice in a concentration camp. She has two children and must decide which one dies.

This situation has its roots in ancient drama and the Bible. There are few examples in cinema of it being used in its literal sense (the taking of a life), other than when mythology or religious subjects are being dealt with.

Possible Scenarios

(1) Assisted suicide. A person is killed to avoid further suffering (Michael Haneke's **L'Amour**). This is done with the consent of the sufferer, but sometimes without it.

(2) In a war situation a loved one may have to be sacrificed in order to protect a larger group. He/she may be slowing down an escape; it could be someone who may 'talk' under torture and therefore represents a risk to the group.

(3) To prevent state interference a father may kill a family member who has committed a crime – keeping it in the family.

(4) Religious/occult crimes. A killer states that the voice of God (or the devil, etc.) spoke to them and commanded

the murder of a loved one. Here we deal with an interesting paradox. We live in a Christian culture in which large sections of the public believe in God and the idea that from time to time God 'speaks' to designated people. But when a killer insists that God spoke to them, we immediately conclude that insanity is the problem. In Arthur Miller's **Crucible** we focus on the hysteria that leads to a witch-hunt and the subsequent killing of members of the community, witches that were formerly 'loved ones'.

(5) Honour killing. Within certain ethnic groups this is still seen as acceptable. Attitudes towards women remain rooted in traditional ideas about gender. A daughter may have dishonoured her family by:

   (a) having a sexual relationship outside of marriage;

   (b) committing adultery;

   (c) refusing to marry a designated partner;

   (d) adopting traits and characteristics alien to the specific group of her peers;

   (e) going against the wishes of parents (particularly those of the father);

   (f) being the victim of a rape.

The responsibility for the honour killing falls upon a male family member: either the father or the brother.

If we broaden the idea to mean giving up or cutting out a loved one, then it is more useful in this context. A family may decide to cut off one of its members entirely as a result of some transgression of a specific family code or law.

EXAMPLE:

The Godfather: Part II (Francis Ford Coppola, 1974)

Michael Corleone orders the murder of his brother, Fredo, because of his disloyalty.

Contemporary cinema and TV (in particular sci-fi and superhero films) remain connected with ancient drama, and therefore many of Polti's original intentions still resonate with these somewhat morally simplified tales.

24. RIVALRY BETWEEN SUPERIOR AND INFERIOR

EXAMPLES:

Amadeus (Miloš Forman, 1984)
The film (based upon a play) chronicles the rivalry between Mozart and Salieri, two composers working under the patronage of an aristocrat. Although Mozart is the better composer, it is Salieri who prospers and seems to be the more successful. But the audience are in no doubt about who is the real superior.

The Servant (Joseph Losey, 1963)
A seemingly loyal servant insinuates himself into a household and gradually takes over the control of the house.

The image I have here is of a horizontal line, with the 'superior' above and the 'inferior' below. (Like many of the situations, I feel this one exists in some kind of parallel universe to the I Ching.)

When Polti's original book was written, the world seemed to be more black and white. Social structures were more rigid, power resided in the upper classes, servants were servants and the working classes for the most part 'knew their place'. The horizontal line was quite rigid, as were the scenarios dealt with – King and Noble, Rich and Poor, Powerful Person and Upstart, Conqueror and Conquered, etc., etc.

Strindberg was one of the first writers to examine the social changes that were already under way by the end of the 19th century, and in **Miss Julie** (1888) he explored a sexual relationship between an aristocratic lady and her servant, in so doing also highlighting the changing politics of gender. The play was banned in Britain for fifty years.

Miss Julie constantly explores the themes of this particular situation, of how the notion of 'superior' and 'inferior' constantly shifts as a result of gender politics in relation to social status. Once Miss Julie is seduced (by the servant), she no longer has the right to be someone superior because she has in fact behaved as an inferior by allowing herself to be seduced by someone from the lower orders. The servant (Jean) dreams of running a hotel and thus elevating himself to a higher position (middle class). The play can function as a masterclass on the subject of situation 24.

In this situation the energy and movement invariably run from 'inferior' up towards 'superior'. The use of the word 'rivalry' implies this movement: a desire to either ascend to the superior position, or to maintain the superior position and prevent someone inferior from usurping its power.

It is in the nature of human beings to try to improve their status, and this urge will often create conflict with others. So this situation is something that all audiences can relate to. We also know instinctively that the status quo can change at any moment, that nothing remains static for long. To quote J. G. Ballard again:

Life is a stage set to be swept away.

This situation was often central to the screwball comedies of the 1930s – films such as **It Happened One Night** (Frank Capra, 1934) or **My Man Godfrey** (Gregory La Cava, 1936), which reflected the disparity of wealth during the Great Depression.

WHERE MIGHT THE SYMPATHIES OF THE AUDIENCE LIE?

(1) Are they rooting for the superior character whose position and status are being threatened by some callow upstart? Does this also signify a change in the social status quo, where the finer, more delicate world is being eroded by a cruder, less aristocratic order? In Terence Rattigan's **The Browning Version** (Mike Figgis, 1994) a classics teacher is forced to retire to make way for a more 'up to date' kind of teacher. The older man can no longer connect with the young pupils and his demise is somehow inevitable, but the play seems to suggest that a wider social change is taking place too. Our sympathies clearly reside with the older teacher, and we are invited to mourn the changes taking place between superior and inferior.

(2) With the underdog we have someone who, after years of deprivation and hardship, is slowly acquiring the power to challenge the superior. The underdog is motivated by ambition, while the superior may be complacent and arrogant, taking their position for granted. We can enjoy observing the shift in balance as the superior is forced to take the protagonist more seriously than before. Inevitably, this leads (in drama

as opposed to life) to a time when the balance is equal, and then comes the expectation of a **REVERSAL OF FORTUNE**.

Human beings compute their own status constantly by factoring in perceptions of inferior/superior, alpha/beta. Within drama, audiences relate to this category on a psychological/personal level.

In a psychological drama the difference between superior and inferior can be in a constant state of flux. The smallest piece of information can immediately alter this fragile balance, like a chess game between two strong players.

Gossip may be used to great effect to alter the group's perception of one of the protagonists.

One of the protagonists may feign inferiority in order to give their opponent a false sense of superiority.

25. ADULTERY – BETRAYAL OF LOVE

```
EXAMPLE:
Arbitrage (Nicholas Jarecki, 2012)
A husband has an affair, which ends when his
mistress dies in a car accident. The police
suspect that he killed the mistress. The wife
and daughter find out. The wife exacts financial
revenge.
```

In the 19th century **ADULTERY** was a cause for scandal. Marriage was held sacred, an inflexible contract totally biased in favour of the male. This was still a time when it was possible for a husband to have his wife committed to a mental hospital if her behaviour was deemed unacceptable to him. Class was a huge issue. Within the upper classes both men and women conducted discreet extra-marital affairs, but in the lower echelons adultery was deemed sinful, particularly for women.

Despite the continued gender imbalance in the 21st century, our attitudes towards marriage and, therefore, adultery have changed enormously. Statistics tell us of the failure of most marriages (in the West), and the single parent is a fact of life. But despite that, there is still a curious holdover from the 19th century in our attitudes to marriage and its sanctity. When marriage is portrayed in drama, it still has within it the idea of permanence, the concept that 'love will keep us together'. The fact that the word 'adultery' has long since lost its potency in daily life does not mean that it is redundant within contemporary drama.

When two people form a relationship, a partnership, a kind of contract to be faithful and truthful to each other, the breaking of that pact is highly emotional. There are many ways in which a loving relationship can be corrupted and then broken, leaving behind dangerous wreckage.

There are many possibilities when it comes to connecting this situation with the others, but first we must decide:

(a) are we primarily interested in the psychology of the situation? A drama about the principal protagonists, the entire drama to be contained within these specific boundaries, i.e. **ADULTERY**? Or

(b) are we more interested in a bigger canvas, where the adultery triggers other events – wars are started, murders committed, children traumatised and loyalties questioned?

When we create a period drama, we invariably superimpose contemporary morality onto it. Thus, if the subject is slavery, or women's rights, or child labour . . . or adultery, we view these themes from a supposedly more enlightened perspective. To write a dramatically 'truthful' period drama, we should really try to immerse ourselves in the generic morality of that period. It's worth remembering this before beginning to write. The enlightened perspective of the present tense often has a counter-effect: it can distance the audience from the narrative, and characters become caricatures.

Looking at Polti's original book, I would say that very few of his categories for **ADULTERY** have much resonance with the 21st century. Gender politics have moved on in that aspect at least. But I have included a few of them because of an interesting trick that can be played with gender clichés – namely, reversing the sexes.

All of these situations are based upon the idea that the protagonist is in a long-term relationship with someone – a partner, husband, wife, etc.

(1) A man has a mistress. He grows tired of her and forms a relationship with a younger man/woman. The relationship has now grown from three people to four. The discarded mistress may have ideas of revenge.

Gender flip

A wife has a lover, grows tired of him and forms a new relationship with a younger man/woman.

(In both cases the official partner has no knowledge of these extra characters, so the idea of revenge often requires letting the innocent party know.)

(2) A husband/wife has a lover, experiences guilt and remorse, and finishes the affair. The discarded lover then creates problems (e.g. **Fatal Attraction**).

The possible scenarios are numerous and complex. Sometimes it is more powerful in film to focus on the psychological state of the main protagonist.

EXAMPLE:

A husband is having an affair. We focus on the wife as she struggles to deal with the situation.

Gender flip

A woman is having an affair. The husband may
suspect something but does nothing because he
doesn't want to lose his wife. She loves her
husband but is consumed by her infatuation with
the new (younger) lover. Everyone struggles to
maintain a normal life, but it becomes more and
more difficult as the affair continues.

THE JILTED LOVER

In **Fatal Attraction** the choice was made to focus on the
husband. He had the affair and then jilted the lover, who
became revengeful. The wife, after initially being upset,
joins forces with the husband to defeat the 'bunny boiler'
psycho ex-lover. The film could just as easily have focused
on the lover and her POV, in which case the portrayal would
have been more sympathetic, as follows:

A woman has an affair with a married man. She becomes
too attached, which scares off the middle-class husband. He
ends the relationship and returns to the comfort of his family. The lover becomes obsessive and crosses over into madness. A victim of love?

We could also have focused on the wife. She discovers her
husband's infidelity through the discarded lover. The perceived threat to her family allows her to support her husband
in fending off the threat . . . but their marriage will never be
the same, and at some future date she may punish him by
beginning an affair of her own and letting him know this.

The intensity of feelings that can be generated by adultery
can lead to extreme behaviour and even madness. In **L'Enfer**
(Claude Chabrol, 1994) a husband suspects that his wife is

having an affair, and this possibility slowly drives him mad. Circumstances sometimes suggest that he is correct in his suspicions, but his wife always denies it. By the end of the film we see that he is now paranoid and dangerous. He has tied up his wife and has a knife. Like all great psychological thrillers, we are left with the possibility that he may be right.

In many societies the punishment for adultery continues to be extreme, particularly towards the woman: honour killings and public humiliations, beatings, etc. In certain Islamic cultures women are still stoned to death for adultery. It is the duty of the dramatist to propose alternative scenarios. In **One Night Stand** (1997) I attempted this at the conclusion of the story by having both couples commit adultery at the same time, thereby neutralising the situation.

26. INCEST

INCEST: *sexual intercourse between people classed as being too closely related to marry each other. (Latin – incestus, meaning impure.) Usually between father and daughter, sometimes between mother and son, sometimes between siblings.*

Incest is wrong because it introduces into the family a notoriously incendiary dynamic – sexual tension – into the mix.
  William Saletan

EXAMPLES:
Festen (Thomas Vinterberg, 1998)
A father has abused a son and daughter, with the knowledge of the mother.

Spanking the Monkey (David O. Russell, 1994)
A teenage son spends summer with his mother and they begin a sexual relationship.

Murmur of the Heart (Louis Malle, 1971)
A bohemian mother takes her young son with her to a resort to meet with her lover. She gets drunk and has sex with her son.

Close My Eyes (Stephen Poliakoff, 1991)
An adult brother and sister who have grown up in separate households begin a sexual relationship.

In Polti's original book he had a category called **ACCIDENTAL CRIMES OF LOVE**. He was referring to situations in which two lovers were unaware of the fact that they were blood relatives, i.e. father–daughter, mother–son, brother–sister.

ACCIDENTAL INCEST

In this situation the lovers are innocent, blameless – there was no intention to commit a crime. But we, the audience, are allowed to be aware of their family ties, and therefore an uncomfortable tension can be developed if desired, because the audience will be alert to the possibilities.

In **Liebestraum** (1991) I created male and female protagonists who never discovered that they were half-brother/sister.

Families are carefully documented within all cultures. Our names place us in carefully delineated family groups – one of the main reasons being the desire to avoid inbreeding. The Bible and other religious books all stress the taboo nature of incest. But in times of war or disaster these safeguards can quickly be destroyed; we are left with no records and, therefore, the possibilities of accidental incest increase dramatically.

Accidental incest also ties in very strongly with the concept of coincidence, the idea that a fragmented family can once again unite, albeit with disastrous results – a kind of family anarchy.

Incest relates entirely to the subject of family, and we are dealing with a very complex set of psychological ideas. Audiences, of course, relate to the subject, but incest is a dark and often taboo subject and is rarely dealt with in cinema, probably for those reasons.

INTENTIONAL INCEST

(1) Father–daughter.

(2) Father–son.

(3) Brother–sister.

(4) Mother–son.

(5) Mother–daughter.

The most common example is between father and daughter, often with the knowledge of the mother and other family members. If there is more than one daughter, the father may transfer from the older sibling to the younger. The daughter may be compliant, believing that this is an expression of love, of favouritism, a special secret between herself and her father.

It may take place in isolated communities or in other situations where there is little communication between the family and the outside world, and is yet another example of how the delicate balances within the family can be corrupted, how sex can be used as a weapon.

> EXAMPLES:
> A fragmented family. The husband leaves the family when the children are infants. They grow up without their father. The daughter, now 18, decides to locate her father. She visits him and they form a relationship that culminates in sex.

If we were to write this story, there would be psychological decisions to be made regarding responsibility and motive. We have to deal with complex ideas about gender, Freudian theories about father–daughter sexuality, love, etc.

Version One

The father meets his daughter, now a sexually
mature 18-year-old. He has not gone through the
process of family evolution with her, has no
memory of her as a child, has no other family
members present (wife, siblings) to remind him of
the barriers, so he sees her not as his daughter
but as someone to be seduced. The daughter thus
becomes a victim of the situation.

Version Two

The daughter, 18, sexually mature, is having
problems in her relationship with her mother,
perhaps issues with her stepfather, etc., etc.
She decides to find her father. She tracks
him down in another town and turns up on his
doorstep. Her own naive sexuality plays a part
in what follows. She needs to see his love for
her and unconsciously begins to seduce him. Of
course, it is the father's responsibility at this
point to demonstrate the appropriate barriers
of behaviour, but he is weak and the absence of
constraint from his family makes it possible for
a sexual relationship to develop between father
and daughter.

Version Three

In similar circumstances (a fragmented family)
a brother and sister may meet as teenagers and
develop a physical relationship.

Incest often involves the silent complicity of other family members. In the case of the father it seems to tie in with a patriarchal idea that somehow he 'owns' his daughters or sons.

MYTHICAL/HISTORICAL EXAMPLES

(1) Oedipus marries a woman he later discovers to be his mother, who hangs herself. Oedipus blinds himself and their children are also punished.

(2) Caligula is rumoured to have had sex with all three of his sisters. (Brother/sister marriages were common during certain periods in ancient history.)

(3) Emperor Claudius married his brother's daughter, Agrippa, changing the law to permit this.

(4) Lucrezia Borgia is rumoured to have had incestuous relationships with her father and her brother.

SOME STATISTICS

- 10–15 per cent of the world's population has had at least one incestuous encounter. Among women the figure is higher – 20 per cent.

- Father–daughter incest is the most highly reported form of incest. However, studies indicate that the most prevalent manifestation is among siblings, in particular older brother–younger sister, where the abuse occurs over a longer period of time and has a higher rate of penetrative sex and violence than in a father–daughter relationship.

- Father–son incest occurs but tends to go unreported, so statistics are rare.

- In India, the close-knit family masks an alarming statistic: more than 70 per cent of those surveyed said they had been abused as a child, over 40 per cent by a family member.
- When the victims reach adulthood, they suffer long-term psychological damage: feelings of low self-esteem, unhealthy sexual activity, contempt for other women, difficulties sustaining relationships, depression, anxiety, substance abuse, and so on.

RECENT EXAMPLE

A three-year-old boy is taken from his family environment because of his father's violent behaviour. He is adopted, then aged 23 finds his biological parents, makes contact and moves in with his mother and 16-year-old sister. The mother dies, and the siblings become lovers and go on to have four children. The couple are prosecuted and jailed, the children put into foster care.

27. DISCOVERY OF THE DISHONOUR
OF A LOVED ONE

EXAMPLES:

Music Box (Costa-Gavras, 1989)
A daughter learns that her father may have been a
Nazi war criminal. The film revolves around her
attempts to deal with the resulting situation.

Vertigo (Alfred Hitchcock, 1958)
A detective is asked by an old friend to
investigate the activities of his wife. He falls
obsessively in love with her, only to discover
that he has been deceived and used to cover up a
murder.

Festen (Thomas Vinterberg, 1998)
A bourgeois Danish family gather together to
celebrate the 70th birthday of the father. The
eldest son chooses this moment to reveal the
incestuous rape of his twin sister by their
father. The assembled family at first refuse to
believe this.

This dramatic situation hinges on the discovery of a dark
secret within a family setting. There are other situations
where a family might collectively know a dark secret but
choose to repress it; this would be altogether different psychologically, but these grey areas are interesting. In **Festen**

the son asks the mother why she did nothing, implying that she knew what was happening.

This is yet another family situation that audiences can relate to. After all, is it ever possible to know someone absolutely, even a family member? A husband and wife may both have had histories before they married and may have told 'edited' versions of these to each other, so there is always the possibility that much more information is hidden than is revealed.

Revelations often appear after a death. Family members become curious about unknown pasts, documents are exposed, journals read, letters examined and uncomfortable truths revealed, which in turn 'dishonour' the memory of the deceased.

EXAMPLE:
Such Good Friends (Otto Preminger, 1971)
After the death of her husband a woman discovers that he has had affairs with other women.

POSSIBLE EFFECTS OF THE DISCOVERY
(1) Love turns to disgust and hatred, and the protagonist is ejected from the family environment; or,
(2) He/she is allowed to stay, albeit with zero status, a non-person who is marginalised. In **Festen** we have the impression that this is the fate of the father.
(3) Love is threatened, and for a period is absent, but then there is adjustment and finally forgiveness. The relationship is tested to its limit, and at first it is not clear whether it can survive. Its survival will depend

entirely on the ability of the 'wronged' party to be
able to forgive and move on. Even if this occurs, we
have the sense (possibly from experience) that there
will always be scars and a shadow cast over what was
previously an unblemished relationship.

The audience will be very involved in the morality of the
situation. Their tolerance is crucial for the drama to be successful. Also, where were their sympathies in the first place?
Are they with the dishonoured or the culprit?

EXAMPLE:
Phoenix (Christian Petzold, 2014)
A female survivor from Auschwitz has had facial
surgery after being shot by a camp guard. On her
return to Berlin she finds her husband, but he
does not recognise her (and believes that his
wife is dead. He asks her to impersonate his wife
so that they can claim the estate of the dead
woman.

In general, we will not tolerate a character who has somehow chosen, without coercion, to do something reprehen-
sible. Crimes against children or women are for the most
part entirely unforgivable. Racial crimes are more complex
because there may be circumstantial factors related to the
group dynamics, and these can be mitigated by genuine
remorse and contrition in characters who have somehow
become more tolerant and humane.

In situation 27 the possibilities for the writer are very
interesting and psychologically complex:

(1) Does the protagonist try to hide the truth? When the truth comes out, does their behaviour imply that they have not come to terms with the past?

(2) Does the protagonist freely offer the truth, taking the risk that it will probably damage their other relationships? In a short story by Elizabeth Bowen a young girl observes as her father confesses to his wife that he has had an affair. Tears are shed and hugs given, and the expectation is of the family surviving and forgiving. But at the end of the story the wife quietly asks the husband when he will be moving out. This comes as a complete shock.

(3) Does the protagonist vehemently deny the accusation of 'dishonour' (as in **Music Box**)? This may result in some kind of trial, either official or within the family. There are only two possible outcomes: the protagonist is either guilty or innocent. Audiences are immediately drawn into these situations. Even when proved guilty, the protagonist may continue to protest innocence, and it will then be up to the individual family members to decide what their feelings are. If we present the protagonist as a decent human being – kind, considerate, a good parent, etc. – it becomes almost impossible for the children to imagine the parent being capable of something awful.

We live in an age when forensic technology is capable of solving crimes from decades earlier, in particular through the use of DNA evidence.

EXAMPLE:

A body is discovered, a woman who went missing
30 years earlier. She has been murdered. The ex-
husband, now remarried with adult children, is
under suspicion. He tells his family that he is
innocent. He is charged, tried and found guilty.
He still protests his innocence. The family now
divides, half of them supporting him, the other
half believing him guilty.

It can be interesting to reverse the sexes in these scenarios
to see the role gender tends to play.

28. OBSTACLES TO LOVE

`Brokeback Mountain` (Ang Lee, 2005)
The love of two cowboys for each other is kept
a secret from their families over a number of
years.

It would seem that love is a very strong and fascinating subject for all audiences. The evidence strongly suggests that women and men see it in very different ways. A love story that has no complications is not particularly interesting in a dramatic context.

Possible Scenarios

DIFFERENCES IN SOCIAL STATUS

From birth we are programmed by our family and environment, so that by adulthood we have developed a strong sense of who we are, where we belong on the food chain and, most importantly, what higher position we may aspire to. Thus, a man/woman may fall in love with a woman/man from a higher social order, which immediately unleashes a long list of possibilities:

(1) Is the 'love' motivated by a desire to climb the social ladder? In which case our sympathies would be with the character whom we feel is being used.

(2) The woman may find his inferior status unattractive, despite being physically aroused by him. In which case she may use him for pleasure and then dump him. Ditto the man.

(3) The family of the 'higher' party could present obstacles to the love. In this case we would assume that the love was genuine and would be rooting for the couple. But in this scenario we often end with the sad realisation that this coupling was somehow doomed from the start. Once the passion of the affair had cooled, there would be an understanding that the two social orders would not be combined.

(4) A man and woman from the same social class may seem a perfect fit, but the ambitions of one or both of them make them realise that the relationship will not work. Marriage (love) is seen as a route to a better place. We, the audience, might see things differently. We see them as perfect for each other; we sense that neither of them will ever find a better partner and we may hope for a later scene in which, after some failed attempts at finding someone better, they come to their senses and reunite, thus creating a whole world again. Audiences like this healing of disunity, and it is the theme of many romcoms.

(5) A variation of this is when the perfect couple part and one of them waits patiently for the other to return, but after a long time loses patience and marries a lesser character. At which point the other comes to their senses and returns, only to discover that they have now missed the boat.

The screenwriter has a multitude of possibilities. As soon as choices are made about personalities within situations – in other words, deciding on the crucial balances that affect the way the audience will interact with the characters and, most importantly, where its sympathies will lie – the story will begin to tell itself.

An interesting wild card in this situation is the power of physical beauty. In stories about love, one character may fall madly in love with another purely because of the physical-beauty factor. This is more pertinent to film than theatre because of the use of the extreme close-up. The camera worships beauty. If we compare a list of the greatest theatre actors with their film counterparts, it is clear how much cinema values physical beauty (in both men and women), far more than is the case with theatre. In theatre actors can continue to act in young parts well into middle age. Their discreet distance from the audience – coupled with careful lighting – can maintain the illusion of youth and beauty. This was never the case in cinema. Arguably, the obsession with youth and beauty in present-day culture has become ridiculous (and all the fault of the close-up).

Be that as it may, the power of beauty on screen is undeniable, and therefore it is a valid factor in screenwriting. This surface beauty, which is embodied by every big movie star, allows characters to transcend many of the obstacles to love. In films we tend to worry less about the future, so blinded are we by screen presence. We did not worry about how Marlon Brando would look as an old man; the same with Brigitte Bardot. We iconise James Dean because he did us the favour of not growing old; the same with Marilyn Monroe.

(6) Sex. Nineteenth-century theatre and literature presented a simplified picture. Once a man had seduced a woman, he lost interest. The woman, on the other hand, became more attached to the idea of love, often becoming obsessive (e.g. Anna Karenina). Obviously, this was coloured by factors like the social status of women, the sanctity of marriage and the gender mechanics of the sexual act itself, something that was rarely discussed or considered. If we are dealing with a screenplay about the 19th century, we can now discuss it from a different perspective, one of relative enlightenment. Sex has to be taken into account because it will probably dominate the initial stages of a love affair. Desire, infatuation and yearning will initially override other considerations.

As I have mentioned several times, it is interesting to reverse gender stereotypes. A woman may have sex with a man and quickly lose interest after the thrill of seduction has passed, while the man falls deeper in love and becomes obsessed.

(7) Ethnicity. The power of family is particularly evident when it comes to the issue of love that wishes to transcend ethnic/tribal boundaries. Often it is the case that decisions about marriage are still being made by the parents, and that going against them may have fatal consequences (as in honour killings). Even if never seen, the presence of family will be felt.

(8) Obstacles created by enemies – ex-lovers, wives, husbands, rivals. The enemy may be hidden.

EXAMPLE:

A woman falls in love with a man. Her best friend
is secretly in love with the same man. The woman
confides everything to her friend, who is then
able to manipulate the situation to her own
advantage, feeding the man negative information
with the ambition of ultimately winning his love.
When we watch this drama, there is usually the
strong sense that in time this will backfire and
true love will win the day. But if the friend
wins the man's affection, the spurned woman can
now plan her revenge, and we move on to another
dramatic situation.

29. AN ENEMY LOVED

Although this is closely related to situation 28, it has one
essential difference: each of the lovers belongs to a separate
group and these groups are at war with each other. In con-
trast, 28 tends to focus on more obvious obstacles: religion,
status, finance, etc.

EXAMPLES:
West Side Story (Robert Wise, Jerome Robbins,
1961)
A young man and woman, associated with different
gangs, fall in love - with tragic results. A
situation as old as **Romeo and Juliet.**

The Night Porter (Liliana Cavani, 1974)
A Jewish concentration camp survivor accidentally
meets her Nazi guard. They feel compelled to
resume their sexual relationship.

Hiroshima Mon Amour (Alain Resnais, 1959)
A French woman has an affair with a German
soldier. Once the Germans are defeated she has
to pay the price and is branded a collaborator.
Her head is shaved and she endures public
humiliation.

Situation 28 also focuses on the reason for the enmity

between the two groups – families or nation states that have
a long history of enmity . . .

EXAMPLES:
A man from group A kills a man from group B.
The group A man then falls in love with a woman
from group B. She then discovers the truth (27 -
DISCOVERY OF THE DISHONOUR OF A LOVED ONE).

Cal (Pat O'Connor, 1984)
Cal, a young IRA man, falls in love with the
widow of a man murdered by his faction.

Gender flip
The Crying Game (Neil Jordan, 1992)
An IRA terrorist falls in love with the wife of a
British soldier who has died after being captured
by the IRA. He eventually discovers that the wife
is a transsexual.

IS BLOOD THICKER THAN WATER?
Love is extremely powerful. Desire is often enhanced by the
perversity of this kind of situation, but in the long run the
influence of family or ethnicity can be volatile, leading to
exceptionally dramatic scenarios.

Loving an enemy may also entail one of the lovers having
to relocate to a hostile environment, which in time may make
life difficult to endure.

30. AMBITION

SELFISHNESS: *a disregard for others, an escalating ruthlessness employed in the pursuit of ambition. It is often a central theme in comedy.*

EXAMPLES:
Sweet Smell of Success (Alexander Mackendrick, 1957)
Two men get involved in a complex story of ambition and betrayal. Both of them will stop at nothing to achieve their goals.

Black Swan (Darren Aronofsky, 2010)
A young, obsessively dedicated dancer finds herself caught up in the dangerously ambitious world of ballet.

See also **Showgirls** (Paul Verhoeven, 1995) and **The Social Network** (David Fincher, 2010).

Here we are focusing on **AMBITION** in its more extreme forms. It is reasonable to assume that we are all ambitious in some way, but when ambition is exposed and other people are forced to interact, it becomes a dramatic situation.

EXISTENTIALISM would have us believe that there is no such thing as a pure act of kindness; everything is evaluated for its long-term usefulness. In polite society we are taught that ambition should be masked, subtle and often portrayed as something else.

In this situation we are focusing on **UNCONTROLLED AMBITION**, **SELFISH AMBITION** and **OBSESSIVE AMBITION**. These are dangerous and often self-destructive traits.

In (9) **DARING ENTERPRISE** we see the ambition as positive because the end result is not selfish; it is for the good of other parties as well as the protagonist (who can bask in the glory of their achievement without recrimination). If the daring enterprise fails, then the protagonist must pay the price and accept the consequences.

In **AMBITION** the protagonist is unaware of virtually anything but the selfish goal. In drama we often associate this with a loss of control, loss of empathy for others, a gradual isolation. In films like **Citizen Kane**, **Scarface** and **The Godfather** the central character begins as charming, intelligent and sympathetic, but ends up isolated, lonely and out of touch with reality.

Ambition, naked or otherwise, can lead to immense wealth. The extremely rich tend to bond together in clubs where they can compare their wealth with characters similar to them. The super-rich, now as ever, have found ways of avoiding isolation and madness by restricting their interactions with lesser mortals. They live in a world where wealth is normal and avoid situations where they might have to question their own moral criminality. These are rich pickings for any screenwriter.

In the late 20th century world leaders like Thatcher and Reagan gave selfishness a respectability. Naked ambition was made acceptable. Films like **Wall Street** (Oliver Stone, 1987) dealt with the financial world, while the **Godfather** series and **Scarface** dealt with crime, but the central characters all had much in common.

In dramatic **AMBITION** it is rare for the protagonist to be able to reverse the psychology, see the error of their ways and become a normal person again. How many times have we heard variations of:

You've changed! I hardly recognise you any more.
    Or:
You no longer seem to care about people. To you they're just numbers, statistics. What's happened to you?

Invariably, this scene would be followed by further distance and isolation as the character continues on a seemingly inevitable path.

But there are subtle variations of this theme. If the partner (wife/husband) or a loyal associate makes the statement, it rarely has a positive impact. If, on the other hand, a more surprising character intervenes, it can have a more positive result. It really depends on what weight this particular situation has on the overall scenario.

    EXAMPLE:
    If the main story is about ambition and the
    central character is ambitious, it is more likely
    that the weight of the ambition will carry the
    day. However, if situation 30 is a facet of a
    wider story in which a character's ambition
    is creating a problem, then the result can be
    different.

GODFATHER: a lesser character's ambition is making waves. After a meeting with the Godfather, the character is persuaded to modify their ambition. But we may have the sense that sooner or later the ambition will reappear and this character will have to be ruthlessly dealt with for not heeding the warning.

The function of drama remains the same as ever: to understand ourselves better by observing a collection of somewhat clichéd behavioural patterns of interaction. We must be careful never to lose contact with a character by describing them in such a way that we no longer recognise ourselves.

31. CONFLICTS WITH POWER

12 Years a Slave (Steve McQueen, 2013)
A 'free' black man is kidnapped into slavery and
battles to survive the cruelty of his owner.

The Insider (Michael Mann, 1999)
A whistle-blower tries to expose the corruption
within the tobacco industry but faces huge
obstacles.

Sophie Scholl: The Final Days (Marc Rothemund,
2005)
During World War II a small group of German
students begins to question the Hitler regime.
Inevitably, this leads to a reaction from the
Gestapo that has fatal consequences.

In its original form, Polti identified this situation as 'Conflicts
with Gods' in which 'Gods' would have been defined as:

*A designated symbolic deity that the population could
revere, obey, thank or blame, thus creating a unity.*

EXAMPLE:
Clash of the Titans (Desmond Davis, 1981)
The 'Mortals' struggle to resist the power of the
gods over their lives.

The invention of gods or God was a politically motivated idea aimed at pointing large populations in the same direction, thus making them easier to unify and, therefore, control. By creating an abstract leader (whom the majority agreed was the boss), it also dispensed with the problematic issues of continuity of power. Mortal leaders were chosen by the gods through theatrical ritual.

When we refer to God and gods in a religious context, we are in fact referring to the politics of power and control, the very stuff of good drama!

At the time of the publication of Polti's book, huge scientific discoveries were already challenging the existence of God as the Creator of life and our world, but drama was slow to absorb these changes in perception. In the 21st century scientific evidence has changed our perceptive landscape to such an extent that religions can function only as a result of faith – in other words, a deeply rooted trust and belief in matters that are without scientific foundation.

How to redefine 'Conflicts with Gods'? If we substitute for 'Gods' any person elevated by the majority of the community to 'godlike' status, we can have interesting variations.

We are also implying a kind of straitjacket, a situation where (unlike (8) **REVOLT**) there is no possibility of a radical change within the status quo and the struggle will be within a contained set of rules.

(1) Hitler, at his peak, was a god to the majority of the German population. To a greater or lesser extent Mao, Stalin and Mussolini were also 'gods'. Their photographs were widely posted in every public

building and individuals were encouraged to display the images in their houses – a pattern common to most religions. What all 'gods' seem to have in common is the use of power and force as an essential element in their status.

(2) Power of society. For hundreds of years the power of the state in the American south was based on slavery. **12 Years a Slave** shows one man's conflict with this 'godlike' power.

(3) Moguls, capitalists and oligarchs. While they are not universally worshipped, within their vast financial empires they wield great power, command respect and are feared. Their financial power gives them control over many lives and families.

EXAMPLE:
Erin Brockovich (Steven Soderbergh, 2000)
Erin Brockovich takes on the Pacific Gas and Electric Company and wins. Based on a true story.

(4) Struggle with a **DEITY**. Any struggle with these 'gods' will involve the fierce loyalty of the deity's followers and disciples. And as with all of the other possible scenarios of situation 31, there is a large element of 'blind faith', something that is hard to turn around.

32. MISTAKEN JEALOUSY

EXAMPLE:

L'Enfer (Claude Chabrol, 1994)
The film is based on an unfinished film by
Henri-Georges Clouzot, which was halted when the
director had a heart attack. A newly married
couple run a hotel. The wife is extremely pretty
and is very friendly and open with everyone she
meets. The husband quickly becomes suspicious and
eventually becomes insane with jealousy, to the
point where he (and, to an extent, the audience)
find it very difficult to differentiate between
truth and fantasy.

JEALOUSY is at its most dangerous at the physical height of a relationship, when either one or both of the players is/are being motivated by their sexual addiction to one another.

It raises interesting ideas about gender, the time-honoured belief among many men that they somehow 'own' their female partner. While this is a male cliché, in some cases it is also true of female attitudes. It frequently leads to physical aggression.

Often the jealousy comes into existence because one of the protagonists is insecure. A classic example: a man marries a beautiful woman. At first he cannot believe his luck (he is not so handsome or rich), and then he begins to question why she would choose him when there were far more interesting suitors around. Soon this turns to suspicion and jealousy.

An insecure lover is tremendously vulnerable to being influenced by others – the insecurity is obvious and visible to anyone wishing to exploit it.

In many cases the energy that goes into jealousy could more usefully be channelled into 'love'. But the truth is that love is very complex, often unfathomable, whereas jealousy is fairly simple and much easier to deal with. Also, there is a perversity in most of us that yearns to prove the negative rather than accept the positive.

Jealousy can frequently be triggered by a small, apparently insignificant event that plants a seed of doubt. It is a particularly interesting category because it deals with the way in which human beings perceive each other.

It is not unusual to have two protagonists who do not really know each other: typically, a man and a woman who find themselves deeply attracted to each other but at the same time have only a sketchy knowledge of each other's personal history and background. What they will have divulged to each other will be selective pieces of information based on ideas of what the other may want to hear. Add to this generic cross-gender mistrust, and the mix can quickly become volatile. It may involve some strategic withholding of the truth or deliberate misleading in order to prevent a negative situation.

Possible Scenarios

A man suspects that his lover is being
unfaithful. He checks up on her and discovers

```
that she occasionally meets another man. He
confronts her, and she admits to the meetings but
insists they are entirely innocent, that the man
is merely a 'friend' from her past. He asks why
she wasn't open about the meetings. She explains
that she felt he would be jealous; she intended
to tell him but then somehow did not, and the
situation compounded itself.
```

While this is a 'believable' answer, it still leaves many possibilities open. The film is probably also withholding the truth at this point in order to develop the drama: quite possibly the audience is torn as to whom to believe.

Male and female responses to this example may vary considerably. We all tell white lies from time to time, and we also understand the insecurities that come with relationships.

```
Finally, she swears her innocence, affirms her
exclusive love for him and begs him to believe
her. He seems to accept her story. BUT . . .
    Both he and the audience now have a shadow of
a doubt planted and the scenario is ready to
develop in a number of potential directions.
```

A crucial strength of cinema (as opposed to theatre) is its ability to observe body language. In the example above, the theatre version would be centred on the dialogue between the couple. In the cinema version, the camera would, at some point, be the POV of the man as he begins to spy on his lover. As he observes her reaction to his questioning, we, the audience, will also begin judging her.

EXAMPLE:

Let us assume, for the moment, that she is telling
the truth and that her liaisons with the 'friend'
are entirely innocent. But when they meet at
a cafe she is very tactile with him; when they
part they hug for longer than seems appropriate.
The explanation could be that he is more like
a 'brother' to her, or that they once had a
relationship and are comfortable with each other's
bodies, but no more than that. It is also true to
say that individuals behave very differently when
in the company of their partners than if they are
outside of that zone. With their partners they
are careful not to be too intimate with others,
avoiding physical contact, etc., whereas outside
that scenario they might be much more physical.
It doesn't mean they are misbehaving; in fact,
they are being more 'normal'.

In **Internal Affairs** (Mike Figgis, 1990), when Andy Garcia's character observes his wife having a meeting with Richard Gere's character, her body language seems to suggest an intimacy that the husband buys into, with terrible consequences. In fact, the wife's actions are innocent. However, when I previewed the film it became clear that the audience had also bought into the suggestive imagery and was beginning to believe that she was less than innocent. The studio was uncomfortable with the ambiguity and suggested changes.

The screenwriter has choices:

(1) to create a scene that conclusively 'proves', one way

or the other, the truth of the situation. In **Othello** we
know the truth about Desdemona, but Othello does not
and is manipulated by Iago;

(2) to reveal some chosen elements of the situation and
withhold others, which puts the audience firmly in the
camp of the jealous protagonist (e.g. **L'Enfer**).

CAUSES OF MISTAKEN JEALOUSY

(1) A chance occurrence/coincidence that sparks a jealous
thought.

(2) A platonic relationship that is assumed to be physical.
As pressure mounts on this 'friendship' (because of the
jealousy), the relationship can in fact become physical.
A perverse element of human behaviour means that
when accused of something we are not guilty of, there
is a temptation to actually commit the crime. It is
also possible that although the friendship seems to be
platonic, the friend may have an agenda that is more
sexual. In this case the woman is innocent, but the
jealous man may be on to something.

(3) **RUMOURS**. A potent dramatic device, something we
are all too familiar with in everyday life. A rumour
may begin innocently, maybe as a result of speculation
about a situation, and then quickly be transmitted as
fact. Each person that passes the rumour on will have
added a personal touch, so that by the time it reaches
the ears of the protagonist, it may well be perceived as
fact. It may also have been deliberately created to cause
damage (e.g. **Othello**). We may use this false-rumour
device in a positive way – to eradicate characters with

whom we do not sympathise. In the digital age the power of the rumour has increased because of the speed and accessibility of false information.

The most interesting thing about this situation is its visceral relationship with the audience. Once we have created a scenario and decided where the sympathy of the audience might be, there are endless possibilities with the psychological drama that ensues.

33. ERRONEOUS JUDGEMENT

The categories listed below appeared in Polti's original book. Hitchcock used many of them in his films. Perhaps his repressive Catholic background contributed to his obsession with guilt and suspicion: as a child he was placed in a prison cell by his father – to teach him a lesson!

(1) Circumstantial evidence suggests that an innocent person is guilty.

EXAMPLE:
Suspicion (Alfred Hitchcock, 1941)
A playboy with a criminal past gets embroiled in a murder case. Everything points to the fact that he was probably the murderer.

(2) The behaviour of an innocent person makes others believe he/she is guilty. (This is a device used frequently in episodic crime stories.) The person may be guilty of something else – adultery, etc. – but not the crime in question.

EXAMPLE:
The Wrong Man (Alfred Hitchcock, 1956)
Circumstances conspire to make a man seem guilty of a crime of which he is innocent. His actions continue to solidify the case against him.

(3) A person deliberately behaves in a guilty fashion
    in order to distract attention from the guilty party,
    possibly a loved one or someone doing valuable work.

(4) The partner or close friend of the guilty person is
    wrongfully accused due to their association with the
    perpetrator. This is often the case in political stories – a
    repressive regime will arrest anyone who was friends
    with a dissident.

(5) An innocent person is accused, someone who intended
    to commit a crime but, in fact, did not. Often, in
    genre stories, the police investigation will find several
    suspects who would have carried out the crime, but
    someone got there before them.

(6) An innocent person thinks they are guilty. This may be
    the result of torture or psychological exploitation.

(7) Or the reverse – a guilty person thinks they are
    innocent, also as a result of torture or psychological
    exploitation (e.g. **The Manchurian Candidate** (John
    Frankenheimer, 1962)).

(8) A witness to a crime remains silent to protect a friend
    or family member.

(9) An enemy throws suspicion onto an innocent party.

(10) A rival in love throws suspicion onto his competitor.

(11) A person struggles to rehabilitate after a miscarriage
    of justice (leading to (3) **REVENGE FOLLOWING A
    CRIME**).

ERRONEOUS JUDGEMENT involves complex moral issues,
but it often comes down to a simple choice: doing the right
thing for oneself and family, or doing the right thing for

wider society. It may also involve an issue which, while technically legal, is on the moral boundary of what is right/wrong.

When an individual becomes aware of a moral dilemma within their organisation, they have a choice of either to ignore it or do something. These days, thanks to the Internet, the news is full of 'whistle-blower' stories – e.g. WikiLeaks, Edward Snowden – but the subtext seems to be about the absence of whistle-blowers. The fact is that within vast organisations – the BBC, the military, the health system, etc. – many people know that bad things are happening but choose to say nothing. The dilemma seems to be one of conflicted loyalty: going against a group of fellow workers, police, military, etc. inevitably has consequences, one of them being the sacrifice of career – (20) **SELF-SACRIFICE FOR IDEALISM**.

Frequently in dramas that hinge on **ERRONEOUS JUDGEMENT** there will be a moment, a window of opportunity to 'do the right thing', which is not acted upon, and it becomes increasingly difficult as time passes to reclaim the opportunity. In films we often focus on these moments: the protagonist is longing to spill some beans; the other person senses this and says, 'Was there something else you wanted to say?' Cut to a close-up of the face, indecision, turmoil, and then, 'It was nothing' – the window of opportunity has again passed.

In storytelling we can then focus on the agony of the protagonist as the guilt mounts, and later, perhaps, because of a second bad thing that occurs, a second opportunity presents itself and the protagonist finally can spill those beans. Entire dramas can be created around these dilemmas.

What I find interesting about **ERRONEOUS JUDGEMENT**

is that it is a situation which creates the possibility of an intense personal drama. When audiences observe disharmony, something that is not right, there is an instinctive response to it: a desire to create harmony again, or at least attempt to make good. While the wider social harmony may still evade us, we like to see the protagonists struggle as they wrestle with their personal morality. This is pure drama.

Possible Scenarios

(1) Witness to a crime but no connection to the victim or the criminal. Doesn't want to get involved so remains silent. Sometime later discovers that an innocent man has been charged with the crime. Still remains silent. The innocent man is from a section of society that the witness dislikes . . . they remain silent.

(2) Witness to a crime committed by an associate or friend. An innocent person is charged with the crime. Out of loyalty remains silent. The severity of the punishment is also a factor. If it is a short term in prison, it is easier to deal with than if the punishment is harsh, perhaps even death. The innocent man pleads for mercy, knows there was a witness, begs him/her to come forward. The moment of confrontation between the victim and the witness can have immense power – they both know the truth and yet the witness still chooses to remain silent. This may be for a number of reasons: peer pressure, a fellow policeman, etc.

(3) Racial issues. So many stories about the Deep South and lynch mobs revolve around the idea of racial

scapegoating. In cultures where racism is profound it is relatively easy to punish the wrong person. Many of the people involved are completely aware of the wrongness of the situation. In a drama we would perhaps want to focus on one individual who struggles to overcome the racism that they have grown up with and tries to 'do the right thing'.

EXAMPLE:
Mississippi Burning (Alan Parker, 1988)
Two FBI agents investigating the disappearance of three civil-rights workers put pressure on a young woman to reveal the truth.

(4) **FAMILY HONOUR**. A rich source of dramatic possibility. A young girl has sex outside marriage. The family honour is at stake, so the story has to be changed so that the girl did not consent, she was raped. In order for this to work, the boyfriend is converted into a criminal rapist, possibly killed. In a recent news story, a very rich Asian teenager killed someone while drunk and driving too fast. The butler was arrested and charged with the crime, with the full knowledge of the rich family – this is similar to one of the episodes in **Wild Tales** (Damián Szifrón, 2014).

EXAMPLE:
Juste avant la nuit (Just Before Nightfall)
(Claude Chabrol, 1971)
A married man murders his lover during a sex game. His remorse causes him to confess, first

to his wife, and then to his best friend, the
husband of the dead woman. They both urge him to
keep silent for the sake of the family. His wife
even justifies the crime as an accident.

(5) **INCEST**. A mother is aware of the father's abuse of a
daughter but does not acknowledge it.

(6) The police are appealing for witnesses to a crime to
come forward. The witnesses are intimidated by the
criminals and keep silent. The criminals overreact
and beat up a witness they suspect will talk. The
witness dies, and this motivates one of the other silent
witnesses to come forward and help the police.

In **Manon des sources** (Claude Berri, 1986) the protagonist has witnessed and participated in terrible deeds against
a naive farmer, ultimately causing his death and the family's
ruin. A generation later he falls in love with the daughter of
the farmer, and is ultimately driven mad by the confluence of
emotions – guilt versus love.

ERRONEOUS JUDGEMENT shares some dramatic psychology with (17) **FATAL IMPRUDENCE**. Both deal with a small
moment in time when a decision is made that then shapes
everything that follows, usually for the worst. There is not
a person alive who has not participated in some version of
this situation. We all carry regrets – 'If only I had spoken up
at that moment' – and so we, the audience, have no problem
relating to this situation.

34. REMORSE

REMORSE: *deep regret or guilt for a wrong committed –*
'They were filled with remorse and shame.'

Our personal morality is entirely the result of the social environment in which we grow up. Whether we like it or not, society forms the moral structure by which we behave. Any action is therefore judged by these social rules. In a court of law, a murderer is assessed by their sanity: if proved sane, then the murder is a conscious crime; if insane, we can forgive because the murderer was judged to be outside of social morality, i.e. an insane person is no longer controlled by social forces.

A child learns the rules of morality first from the family environment and then the wider society. The transition from the first environment to the second is complex: contradictions become apparent and the young individual has to begin making personal judgements about right and wrong.

REMORSE is a very strong subject because it connects everyone to their mother culture. As a dramatic device it is powerful, perhaps more so than in real life.

Once we have done something 'bad', we can never rid ourselves of the memory of that deed, and as time passes and death approaches, this memory becomes a cancer, and with it comes an overwhelming need to unburden oneself and show . . . **REMORSE.**

When Polti's book was first published in the mid-19th century, it's fair to say that Western religion was still an extremely potent moral force. A general belief in the idea of heaven and hell went a long way towards shaping the idea of remorse – in other words, a fear of punishment in the after-life. As we are now firmly into the 21st century, we clearly need to reassess the idea of remorse as a dramatic force.

The existentialist movement, which emerged after World War II, had a powerful influence on cinema. We were presented with characters who seemed to have a complete detachment from the conventions of generic morality. Characters were often drifters who didn't seem to have strong family bonds and had lost all connection with religion.

Cinema quickly converts this dangerous existentialism into a moral plot issue.

The first American script that I worked on was called **The Hot Spot**. Adapted from the novel by Charles Williams, it tells the story of a bank robber, a drifter who arrives in a small Texas town with the idea of robbing a bank. Which he does, but meanwhile he has become involved with a young woman and then decides to save the life of a tramp rather than fleeing with the stolen money, etc., etc. When I was doing the rounds of the studios, raising money for the film, I found myself in the plush offices of a famous old-school producer, who asked me a simple question: 'Why is Madox robbing the bank?' I realised the answer was important but struggled to come up with the goods. 'Because . . . he's a bank robber!' The

executives looked at each other, and then one
of them took pity on my inexperience. 'Does his
mother have cancer?' This really confused me, and
I wondered if some detail of the original script
had eluded me, so I shook my head. Another of
the executives added, 'We mean, is he robbing the
bank to pay for his mother's treatment?' 'Like
Robin Hood,' added another. The famous producer,
clearly a wise guy with a sense of humour, spoke.
'So why is he robbing the bank?' I thought for
a while and then answered, 'Because he's a bank
robber, that's what he does.'

In retrospect I see that they were right.
I cannot think of a single example of an
existentialist plot in a film that was a success
at the box office. However, there are numerous
examples of characters who are introduced as
existential and then, in the course of the drama,
are somehow sucked back into the framework of
the moral culture, at which point they become
candidates for **REMORSE**, often because they have
feelings for another human being.

EXAMPLE:
Casablanca (Michael Curtiz, 1942)
An American expatriate who runs a bar in Morocco
changes from a cynical lone wolf into a Nazi
resister.

VARIATIONS

(1) Remorse for a crime undiscovered. As time passes, the
    crime remains buried, but the protagonist begins to

realise the damage and heartbreak that it has caused, possibly over generations. He tries to make good the situation by helping the unaware victim of the crime. This opens up the situation and may ultimately lead to a revelation: the exposing of the protagonist.

EXAMPLE:

Manon des sources (Claude Berri, 1986)
Ugolin falls in love with a beautiful shepherdess and consequently is destroyed by remorse because he was responsible for the death and ruin of her father.

(2) Remorse for a political crime. The protagonist kills someone in the name of a political ideal. At the time of the killing they are filled with the unshakeable zeal of a believer. Time passes and the world changes, the zeal fades, and they are left with the reality that a life has been taken, leaving behind sadness and tragedy. The protagonist wrestles with their conscience and has to make a decision. The truth and reconciliation trials in South Africa after the apartheid regime was overthrown are a pertinent example of this.

(3) Remorse for the killing (undetected) of a spouse. The death is made to look accidental and the killer then carries on with his life, interacting with other family members. What is so intense about this scenario is the close intimacy of the situation, to be constantly reminded of the victim by the physical traits of the children, daughters or sons who may grow up to resemble the late spouse. In my third film, **Liebestraum**

(1991), I constructed a plot around this idea. Nick Kaminsky is united with a mother he has never met. She is dying of cancer and has only a few days left. Nick never met his father, who died before he was born. In the course of the film we discover that his father was murdered while having an affair with a married woman. Nick's mother has never met her son as an adult, and he bears an uncanny resemblance to his dead father. This forces his mother into an extreme state of memory confrontation and we finally realise that she was the killer.

(4) The killing of a spouse by two people. A wife has a lover, and the two of them arrange to kill the husband. This scenario often comes without remorse (e.g. **The Postman Always Rings Twice**, **Body Heat**, **Double Indemnity**) because the purpose of the drama is the **DOUBLE CROSS**, but in a story like **Thérèse Raquin** (Emile Zola, 1867) it is at its most effective as a device. Thérèse and her lover plot to kill her husband. After his death, circumstances contrive to make them marry each other. The marital bed becomes a terrifying landscape where every night they are forced to confront what they have done. Each plots to kill the other, but when they simultaneously realise this they decide instead to commit suicide. The French seem particularly good at this kind of emotional torturing of the soul.

(5) Remorse for unfaithfulness. One partner has been unfaithful in the past, but it remains a secret. Now the marriage is thriving – children, a good job, nice

house, etc., etc. But for the unfaithful partner the remorse is something that increases as the marriage gets better and better. He/she now has to make a decision: (a) to unburden themselves, to confess to this past indiscretion, which may have a bad result and ultimately destroy the marriage; on the other hand, the protagonist may feel that this happy marriage is not real because of the lie. Or (b) to repress the truth in order to maintain the status quo, the happiness of the family, etc. This requires great personal strength and a perversely unselfish course of action, but it will leave the protagonist isolated and somewhat lonely.

(6) Remorse for a desire which is unfulfilled. A man is secretly in love with a woman. She is aware of this and waits for the love to be declared, but the man always falters, scared of rejection. The love remains unspoken for years, by which time it is too late and events have moved on.

EXAMPLE:
In the Mood for Love (Wong Kar-wai, 2000)
A man and a woman rent rooms next to each other in a boarding house in Hong Kong. Both are married to unfaithful partners. They fall in love but never manage to articulate their feelings to each other.

Characters who suffer from remorse are burdened. They cannot present themselves in an open way to their peers and family. They carry an unarticulated sadness that increases incrementally as time passes.

35. RECOVERY OF A LOST ONE

EXAMPLE:

The Searchers (John Ford, 1956)
A young girl is abducted by Comanches. Her
immediate family are killed, but an uncle and her
half-brother begin a long search for her. During
the course of the film it becomes clear that even
if they do find her, it would probably be kinder
to kill her. The feeling among her relatives is
that she will have been 'contaminated' by sexual
contact with Comanche 'bucks' and will have 'gone
native', never to be a white girl again. Up until
the very end it seems possible that the character
played by John Wayne intends to do this.

This situation is again rooted in family and the extended
family – the desire to maintain the unity of the family.
Everyone can understand the grief that comes from losing
a loved one, so audiences respond well to the unity of the
family being restored. The emotional scale of the situation
is vast:

(1) Someone seemingly lost for ever, with no hope of
being seen again.

(2) A person abducted, kidnapped by terrorists. There's a
ransom demand. In the present political climate this
has become very common, and built into this is the
knowledge that the abducted person may be executed.

(3) A loved one separated by a natural disaster or war. In
recent years we have witnessed two massive tsunamis.
In the aftermath of both, survivors desperately tried
to find family members (e.g. **The Impossible** (J. A.
Bayona, 2012)). In war situations communications
become almost impossible and families become
separated.

(4) Forced adoption. Parents or close relatives try to find
children stolen from their families at birth.

EXAMPLE:
Philomena (Stephen Frears, 2013)
An Irish woman searches for the son taken away
from her because she was unmarried.

This situation can function towards the end of the drama,
one in which the solving of the enigma, the tracking down
and finally the recovery of the missing loved one all form a
neat scenario. We end with collective happiness and are not
expected to examine the future.

If, on the other hand, we place the situation closer to the
beginning or middle of the drama, we have an entirely different and more complex situation to deal with as we focus on
how the loved one comes to terms with the situation.

EXAMPLE:
Olivier, Olivier (Agnieszka Holland, 1992)
A small boy goes missing. Ten years later he is
found living rough in Paris. His mother brings
him back into the family, with catastrophic
results.

After the joy of reconciliation passes, a period of reassessment and change must inevitably follow.

EXAMPLE:

Room (Lenny Abrahamson, 2015)
A mother and small child finally manage to escape from their abductor. At first they are happy to be free, but then it becomes increasingly difficult to deal with 'reality'. The mother's father finds it impossible to relate to her son, who is the result of her rape by the abductor. Society questions why she did not try harder to escape. She has a mental breakdown.

36. LOSS OF A LOVED ONE

EXAMPLES:

The German Sisters (Margarethe von Trotta, 1981)
The film is loosely based upon the Baader-
Meinhof movement. Two sisters have different
views on how to bring about political change.
One becomes a terrorist, the other a journalist.
The terrorist is captured and imprisoned. Her
sister works tirelessly to help her, at great
cost to her own personal life. She takes a much
needed holiday with her boyfriend to try to
save the relationship. While they are away, in
a bar she spots an image of her sister on a TV
news flash but is unable to understand what is
being said about her. Rushing back to her hotel
she discovers that her sister has apparently
committed suicide. The moment she sees the TV is
pure cinema at its very best.

Don't Look Now (Nicolas Roeg, 1973)
Following the tragic death of their only
daughter, a husband and wife go to Venice to
make a new start. But the loss of their child
literally haunts them and they realise it is
impossible to escape the past. The film ends with
the loss of another 'loved one' - the husband -
though there is the sense that a child has been
conceived to replace the daughter.

By 'loved one' we mean someone who is loved, as opposed to just a family member. Within families, individuals may form bonds with someone unique and special, someone sincerely loved. Everyone in the audience will have either experienced this or else knows that it will inevitably happen to them. As such, this situation is a very powerful weapon in the writer's arsenal. Whatever the response of the protagonist to the loss of a loved one, the audience will have a visceral connection to the scenario.

This is extremely dark territory and it is trivialised in many films, being used as the justification for killing sprees and revenge without any real exploration of the deeper psychology that is part of grief and mourning. Cinema and its graphic tools have from the outset amplified the physical/visual aspects of death – torn flesh, blood gushing, etc. Add to that the use of sound to amplify the impact of a bullet hitting flesh and we can see that the movies have grossly theatricalised death, which has also had the effect of diminishing the power of grief.

Possible Scenarios

(1) Witnessing the death of a loved one but being powerless to prevent it, implying some kind of hostile situation where force is being used. Within most war stories there is an infinite number of grim variations of this situation.

(2) Politics/secrecy. A scenario that results in the death of the innocent loved one. A former Mafia member testifies against his gang members. They kill his loved

one, firstly as revenge, secondly as a warning to others
not to do the same.

(3) Discovering the death of a loved one via a third party.
This puts the messenger into a very difficult situation.
Often the news will be met with complete disbelief –
'There must be a mistake, it's not possible.'

As with all of the situations, its placement within the drama
is of great significance:

(1) Beginning: in **Don't Look Now** we begin with the
harrowing death of a child. The narrative is then built
around the grieving parents, with the theme of death
ever present. In François Ozon's **The New Girlfriend**
(2014) the death of a young woman leads the woman's
husband and her best friend to embark on a strange,
erotic relationship.

   QUESTIONS: Can the protagonists come to terms
with the grief? Can they adjust, make a new life?
How much damage has been done to the survivors?
Ultimately, is the struggle too much?

(2) Middle: we chart the events leading up to the loss and
then follow the aftermath. By placing the event in
the middle we may also lessen its impact, and it may
become one of several powerful elements within a
bigger picture, say in a war situation.

(3) End: by placing the event at the end of the drama, it
will inevitably add weight. Moreover, it will ask specific

moral questions. We still have an innate idea that
there is a price to be paid. For example, a person leads
a selfish life and then finds true love and becomes a
reformed character, before their demise.

THE FILM CHART

8½: 8, 11, 12, 19, 22, 25, 27, 30 (8)

Alive: 6, 7, 9, 21, 34, 35, 36 (7)

All About Eve: 7, 12, 18, 23, 24, 30 (6)

Amadeus: 3, 5, 7, 11, 12, 13, 22, 24, 30, 31, 34, 36 (12)

Anna Karenina: 7, 13, 17, 18, 22, 25, 28, 36 (8)

Anything for Her: 2, 5, 6, 7, 9, 12, 18, 21, 31, 33, 35 (11)

Apartment, The: 12, 18, 24, 25, 27, 28, 30, 35 (8)

Apollo 13: 2, 6, 9, 23, 30, 35 (6)

Arbitrage: 3, 4, 6, 12, 17, 25, 30, (7)

Argo: 2, 3, 5, 6, 8, 9, 10, 12, 24, 31, 35 (11)

Ascent, The: 1, 3, 5, 6, 7, 8, 9, 12, 13, 17, 20, 23, 31, 34, 36 (15)

Ashes and Diamonds: 2, 5, 8, 9, 17, 20, 31, 36 (8)

Audition: 2, 3, 10, 11, 16, 17, 28, 35 (8)

Battle of Algiers, The: 3, 5, 8, 20, 31 (5)

Belle de Jour: 5, 9, 11, 17, 19, 22, 25, 28, 29 (9)

Best Intentions: 12, 21, 24, 28, 30 (5)

Betrayal: 4, 23, 24, 25, 27, 28, 33 (7)

Black Swan: 4, 7, 11, 12, 16, 19, 21, 24, 30, 31 (10)

Blade Runner: 3, 5, 8, 9, 11, 23, 24, 28, 29, 31, 34, 36 (12)

Blue Velvet: 1, 2, 5, 7, 9, 10, 11, 16, 17, 18, 19, 27, 28, 35 (14)

Body Heat: 5, 9, 11, 12, 15, 17, 18, 22, 25, 27, 28, 30, 31 (13)

Bond – From Russia with Love: 2, 3, 9, 11, 12, 24, 28, 29, 30, 31, 35 (11)

Bond – Goldfinger: 2, 3, 6, 9, 10, 11, 12, 17, 18, 23, 29, 30, 31, 33, 35 (15)

Bond – Moonraker: 2, 3, 6, 9, 10, 11, 12, 17, 18, 23, 29, 30, 31, 33, 35 (15)

Bond – Spectre: 2, 3, 4, 6, 9, 10, 11, 12, 17, 18, 23, 28, 30, 31, 35 (15)

Bonnie and Clyde: 3, 5, 6, 8, 9, 12, 13, 17, 28, 30, 31, 36 (12)

Breathless: 5, 23, 27, 28, 31, 36 (6)

Brief Encounter: 18, 21, 23, 28, 36 (5)

Browning Version, The: 1, 4, 7, 20, 24, 25, 27, 31, 34 (9)

Butch Cassidy and the Sundance Kid: 2, 3, 5, 9, 12, 17, 22, 31 (8)

Casablanca: 2, 5, 6, 8, 9, 12, 18, 20, 22, 28, 31, 32, 34, 35, 36 (15)

Chinatown: 3, 4, 7, 11, 12, 13, 17, 26, 27, 28, 30, 31, 36 (13)

Citizen Kane: 11, 12, 24, 30, 31 (5)

Conformist, The: 3, 5, 11, 12, 17, 23, 30, 31, 33 (9)

Conversation, The: 5, 8, 9, 11, 17, 30, 31 (7)

Cool Hand Luke: 1, 2, 3, 5, 7, 8, 9, 12, 13, 17, 20, 24, 27, 31, 35, 36 (16)

Damage: 6, 7, 13, 14, 17, 22, 25, 27, 28, 33, 34, 36 (12)

Dark Knight Rises, The: 2, 3, 7, 8, 16, 20, 30 (7)

Deerhunter, The: 2, 5, 6, 7, 9, 13, 16, 17, 18, 23, 28, 31, 34, 35, 36 (15)

Deliverance: 3, 6, 9, 10, 17, 24 (6)

Diabolique: 3, 7, 9, 11, 12, 15, 16, 23, 25, 30 (10)

Die Hard 1: 2, 3, 6, 9, 10, 12, 14, 17, 18, 21, 24, 30, 31, 35 (14)

Die Hard 2: 2, 3, 6, 7, 9, 10, 12, 17, 18, 21, 24, 30, 31, 33, 35 (15)

Dog Day Afternoon: 8, 9, 12, 17, 28, 31, 36 (7)

Dolce Vita, La: 5, 11, 23, 28, 36 (5)

Don't Look Now: 6, 11, 16, 17, 18, 19, 35, 36 (8)

Double Indemnity: 2, 3, 5, 11, 12, 14, 15, 17, 18, 22, 25, 28, 30, 34 (14)

Elvira Madigan: 5, 7, 8, 9, 13, 17, 22, 23, 28, 31, 36 (11)

L'Enfer: 1, 3, 10, 11, 15, 16, 18, 23, 25, 27, 28, 32, 34, 36 (14)

Ex Machina: 8, 11, 12, 17, 23, 31 (6)

Fargo: 3, 5, 10, 12, 13, 14, 17, 23, 24, 30, 31, 34 (12)

Fatal Attraction: 1, 3, 5, 6, 10, 15, 16, 17, 22, 25, 27, 28 (12)

Festen: 3, 4, 7, 11, 13, 14, 16, 19, 26, 27, 33, 34, 36 (13)

Force Majeure: 4, 13, 27, 28, 30, 33, 34 (7)

Forrest Gump: 2, 6, 7, 9, 18, 20, 21, 28, 35, 36 (10)

Fucking Amal: 1, 2, 5, 7, 9, 13, 22, 23, 27, 28, 29, 34, 35, 36 (14)

Fugitive, The (1947): 2, 5, 8, 10, 12, 17, 29, 31 (8)

Gladiator: 2, 3, 5, 6, 7, 8, 9, 10, 12, 14, 24, 30, 31, 36 (14)

Godfather I, II and III, The: 1, 3, 4, 12, 13, 14, 17, 21, 23, 24, 27, 28, 30, 31 (14)

Goodfellas: 5, 12, 13, 17, 24, 27, 30, 31 (8)

Graduate, The: 9, 17, 27, 28, 34, 35, 36 (7)

Grand Budapest Hotel, The: 2, 3, 5, 6, 7, 8, 9, 11, 12, 13, 21, 30, 31, 33, 35, 36 (16)

Guns of Navarone, The: 2, 3, 6, 7, 9, 20, 23, 24, 27, 34 (10)

Heroes of Telemark, The: 2, 6, 9, 20 (4)

Hill, The: 3, 7, 8, 17, 20, 24, 31, 33, 34 (9)

Immortals: 1, 3, 6, 8, 10, 11, 12, 13, 17, 20, 23, 24, 28, 29, 30, 31, 33, 35 (18)

In the Bedroom: 2, 3, 4, 6, 7, 8, 10, 13, 17, 28, 31, 33, 36 (13)

In the Heat of the Night: 3, 5, 9, 11, 18, 24, 31 (7)

In the Mood for Love: 18, 21, 23, 25, 27, 28, 34, 36 (8)

Inception: 1, 2, 3, 5, 9, 10, 11, 12, 19, 21, 24, 31, 33, 35, 36 (15)

Insider, The: 2, 3, 5, 7, 8, 9, 12, 13, 20, 24, 31, 33, 34 (13)

Internal Affairs: 3, 5, 10, 12, 16, 19, 24, 25, 27, 30, 31, 32, 35 (13)

Invasion of the Bodysnatchers: 5, 9, 10, 11, 13, 16, 23 (7)

It Happened One Night: 5, 8, 9, 12, 13, 18, 22, 28, 32, 35 (10)

It's a Wonderful Life: 2, 6, 7, 12, 21, 30, 31, 35 (8)

Ju Dou: 2, 3, 4, 5, 6, 7, 12, 13, 15, 17, 22, 25, 26, 27, 28, 36 (16)

Klute: 2, 9, 11, 28, 35 (5)

Lady Eve, The: 1, 3, 7, 9, 11, 12, 17, 18, 22, 27, 28, 29, 30, 34, 35 (15)

Leaving Las Vegas: 1, 2, 5, 7, 11, 18, 28, 34, 35, 36 (10)

Leviathan: 3, 5, 6, 7, 8, 10, 12, 17, 24, 25, 27, 30, 31, 34, 36 (15)

Liebestraum: 3, 4, 11, 15, 16, 17, 18, 19, 22, 25, 26, 27, 28, 35 (14)

Lifeboat: 1, 2, 3, 6, 8, 11, 12, 21, 24, 31, 33 (11)

Long Day's Journey into Night: 4, 13, 14, 30, 34 (5)

Rear Window: 2, 9, 12, 17, 28 (5)

Règle du jeu, La: 3, 11, 15, 17, 18, 22, 23, 24, 25, 27, 28, 32, 33, 36 (14)

Reine Margot, La: 1, 2, 3, 4, 5, 6, 7, 8, 9, 12, 13, 14, 17, 23, 24, 26, 28, 29, 30, 31, 33, 35, 36 (23)

Repulsion: 16, 17, 19 (3)

Revenent, The: 3, 5, 6, 9, 23, 33, 36 (7)

Rome Open City: 3, 5, 6, 7, 8, 9, 10, 12, 17, 20, 23, 31, 33, 34, 36 (15)

Room: 6, 7, 8, 9, 10, 13, 21, 27, 33, 35, 36 (11)

Rosemary's Baby: 10, 11, 12, 19, 30, 31, 35 (7)

Se7en: 2, 3, 6, 7, 10, 11, 12, 16, 17, 31, 36 (11)

Searchers, The: 2, 3, 5, 6, 7, 9, 10, 12, 13, 23, 27, 35, 36 (13)

Serpico: 3, 5, 8, 9, 13, 20, 31 (7)

Servant, The: 8, 11, 12, 13, 24, 30, 31 (7)

Silence of the Lambs, The: 2, 3, 5, 9, 10, 11, 16, 17, 24, 30, 31, 35 (12)

Silver Linings Playbook: 2, 12, 16, 28, 35 (5)

Some Like It Hot: 2, 5, 9, 11, 17, 28, 31 (7)

Son of Saul: 5, 6, 7, 8, 12, 18, 21, 23, 35, 36 (10)

Sophie's Choice: 5, 6, 7, 10, 11, 16, 23, 27, 28, 32, 34, 36 (12)

Star Wars: The Empire Strikes Back: 1, 2, 6, 7, 8, 9, 10, 11, 12, 13, 19, 23, 28, 31, 34, 35 (16)

Story of Adele H., The: 5, 7, 12, 16, 22, 28 (6)

Sunset Boulevard: 7, 11, 12, 16, 17, 18, 28 (7)

Sweet Smell of Success: 3, 12, 13, 24, 27, 28, 30, 31, 36 (9)

Taxi Driver: 2, 3, 5, 9, 16, 20, 28, 35 (8)

That Obscure Object of Desire: 1, 7, 8, 11, 12, 18, 19, 27, 28 (9)

Third Man, The: 3, 5, 9, 11, 12, 27, 30, 31 (8)

Thelma & Louise: 3, 5, 8, 9, 12, 17, 22 (7)

There Will Be Blood: 1, 2, 3, 4, 6, 7, 9, 12, 13, 14, 15, 16, 17, 24, 30, 31, 33 (17)

Thérèse Raquin: 2, 3, 4, 7, 12, 15, 16, 17, 22, 25, 27, 28, 30, 36 (14)

Time Code: 2, 3, 12, 15, 17, 18, 22, 24, 25, 27, 28, 30, 34, 36 (14)

Titanic: 2, 6, 7, 9, 12, 22, 24, 28, 30, 35, 36 (11)

Touch of Evil: 2, 3, 9, 10, 11, 12, 17, 24, 28, 30, 31, 33, 35 (13)

Train, The: 5, 6, 7, 22, 25, 28, 31, 35, 36 (9)

Twelve Angry Men: 2, 3, 8, 11, 24, 31, 33 (7)

Unfaithful: 15, 17, 22, 25, 27, 35 (6)

Unforgiven: 2, 3, 5, 8, 9, 12, 24, 31 (8)

V is for Vendetta: 1, 2, 5, 6, 7, 8, 9, 10, 11, 12, 17, 20, 23, 31, 34, 35, 36
    (17)

Vertigo: 2, 3, 6, 9, 11, 16, 19, 27, 28, 34, 36 (11)

Wall Street: 3, 6, 7, 8, 12, 13, 17, 20, 23, 24, 27, 30, 31, 33, 34 (15)

West Side Story: 1, 3, 5, 6, 9, 13, 17, 22, 27, 28, 29, 31, 36 (13)

Woman Next Door, The: 2, 13, 15, 16, 17, 18, 22, 23, 25, 28, 35, 36 9 (12)

Written on the Wind: 2, 3, 4, 6, 12, 13, 14, 15, 16, 17, 22, 24, 25, 27, 28,
    30, 31, 32, 33, 34, 36 (21)

Wrong Man, The: 2, 5, 6, 7, 11, 18, 33 (7)

Grids overleaf for you to continue . . .

FILM	1	2	3	4	5	6	7	8	9	10	11	12	13	14	15	16

17	18	19	20	21	22	23	24	25	26	27	28	29	30	31	32	33	34	35	36

FILM	1	2	3	4	5	6	7	8	9	10	11	12	13	14	15	16

7	18	19	20	21	22	23	24	25	26	27	28	29	30	31	32	33	34	35	36

1

SUPPLICATION

HUMILITY / SHAME / REMORSE

2

DELIVERANCE

SURPRISE / RESOLUTION / INTEGRATION

5

THE PURSUED

THE OUTSIDER / THE FUGITIVE / THE UNDER-DOG / CONSPIRACY THEORIES

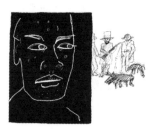

6

DISASTER

TRAGEDY / LOSS / SURVIVAL / ADAPTING / HUMILITY

3

REVENGE FOLLOWING A CRIME

PASSION/ANGER/
OBSESSION/BALANCE

4

REVENGE CONTAINED WITHIN A FAMILY

DARK SECRETS/INCEST/
INSANITY

7

CRUELTY & MISFORTUNE

HUMILIATION/
INHUMANITY/INJUSTICE

8

REVOLT

COURAGE/
DIRE CONSEQUENCES

9

DARING ENTERPRISE / BRAVE ADVENTURE

A PROBLEM/A PLAN/ HIGH RISK

10

ABDUCTION

ENIGMA/POWER/ VULNERABILITY

13

ENMITY OF KINSMEN / FAMILY AT WAR

BITTERNESS /IMPLACABLE/ INGRAINED

14

RIVALRY OF KINSMAN

CLAUSTROPHOBIA/DESIRE

11

THE ENIGMA

MYSTERY/TASK/TEST

12

OBTAINING

**CUNNING/IMPROVISATION/
AMBITION**

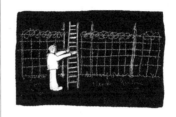

15

MURDEROUS
ADULTERY/CRIMES
OF PASSION

**INTRIGUE/SEDUCTION/
JEALOUSY/
DOUBLE-CROSS/REVENGE**

16

ALTERED STATES/
MADNESS

**OBSESSION/FIXATION/
LOSS OF CONTROL**

17

FATAL
IMPRUDENCE/
THE GAMBLER

18

COINCIDENCE

**FATE/KARMA/
INEVITABILITY**

21

SELF-SACRIFICE
FOR FAMILY

**NOBLE/BRAVE/SELFLESS/
LOVING**

22

EVERYTHING
SACRIFICED FOR
PASSION

**OBSESSION/MADNESS/
RECKLESSNESS**

19

DREAM STATE

**SURREALISM/TRUTH/
ESCAPE/FANTASY/HORROR/
SENSUALITY**

20

SELF-SACRIFICE
FOR IDEALISM

**NOBLE/PROUD/
STUBBORN/BRAVE/
OBSESSED**

23

NECESSITY OF
SACRIFICING
LOVED ONES

**TRAGEDY/NIGHTMARE/
GUILT/SELF-LOATHING**

24

RIVALRY BETWEEN
SUPERIOR &
INFERIOR

**ARROGANCE/HUMILITY/
RESENTMENT/SNOBBERY/
CHAUVINISM/SEXISM**

25

ADULTERY /
BETRAYAL OF LOVE

**COMEDY/TRAGEDY/GUILT/
SEX/BOREDOM/REMORSE**

26

INCEST

**CONTROL/LOVE/SECRETS/
ABUSE/GUILT/FAMILY/
ISOLATION/CONFUSION**

29

AN ENEMY LOVED

**TRAGEDY/INFRACTION/
INFLEXIBILITY**

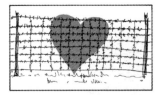

30

AMBITION

**SELFISH DISREGARD/
RUTHLESS/ALIENATION/
BLINKERED**

27

DISCOVERY OF THE DISHONOUR OF A LOVED ONE

BETRAYAL/FAMILY/TRAGEDY

28

OBSTACLES TO LOVE

FRUSTRATION/ INTRIGUE/PASSION

31

CONFLICTS WITH POWER

POWER/ISOLATION/ POLITICS/BLIND FAITH/ MASS HYSTERIA

32

MISTAKEN JEALOUSY

OBSESSION/PARANOIA/ INTRIGUE/DESTRUCTION/ TRUST/CONFUSION

33

ERRONEOUS
JUDGEMENT

**GUILT/CONSCIENCE/
SACRIFICE MORALITY/
FRIENDSHIP**

34

REMORSE

**DENIAL/GUILT/
CONSCIENCE/CONFESSION/
CHANGE**

35

RECOVERY OF A
LOST ONE

**SUSPENSE/FRAGILITY/
EMOTION/ENIGMA/
CAUTION/SUSPICION**

36

LOSS OF
A LOVED ONE

**POWERLESSNESS/GRIEF/
INSANITY/GUILT/
TRAGEDY/ACCEPTANCE**